הגדה של פסח

THE PASSOVER HAGGADAH

A baroque title page depicting Moses and Aaron, above, and the Sacrifice of Isaac, below. Sulzbach, Bavaria, 1711 (JTSAL).

הגדה של פסח

THE PASSOVER HAGGADAH

WITH HEBREW AND ENGLISH
TRANSLATION ON FACING PAGES

Introduction and Commentary
Based on the Studies of E. D. Goldschmidt

Edited by Nahum N. Glatzer

Including Readings on the Holocaust
With Illustrations from the Earliest Printed Haggadot

SCHOCKEN BOOKS · NEW YORK

Library of Congress Cataloging in Publication Data
Jews. Liturgy and ritual.
The Passover Haggadah.
1. Jews. Liturgy and ritual.   Haggadah—Commentaries.
I. Glatzer, Nahum Norbert, 1903—   II. Goldschmidt,
Ernst Daniel.   III. Sloan, Jacob.   IV. Title.
BM675.P4Z555258   1979   296.4'37   79-401
ISBN 0-805-20880-1

Manufactured in the United States of America

Grateful acknowledgment is made to the following for permission to reprint previously published material:

Excerpt from *Anne Frank: The Diary of a Young Girl.* Copyright 1952 by Otto Frank. Reprinted by permission of Doubleday & Company, Inc.

Excerpt from Jacob Glatstein, ed., *Anthology of Holocaust Literature* copyrighted and reprinted courtesy of The Jewish Publication Society of America.

A selection from *The Tiger Beneath the Skin* by Zvi Kolitz. Copyright 1947 by Creative Age Press, Inc. (now a division of Farrar, Straus & Giroux, Inc.). Copyright renewed 1974 by Zvi Kolitz. Reprinted with the permission of Farrar, Straus & Giroux, Inc.

A selection from *Night* by Elie Wiesel. Translated from the French by Stella Rodway. Copyright © 1958 by Les Editions de Minuit. English translation copyright © 1960 by MacGibbon & Kee. Reprinted with the permission of Hill & Wang, a division of Farrar, Straus & Giroux, Inc.

PUBLISHER'S NOTE

The Hebrew text of the present Haggadah is based on traditional versions, except for a few minor changes based on the annotation by Rabbi Elijah, the Gaon of Vilna, and on ancient sources. Brackets are used to indicate passages that, though customarily recited, are not part of the original text, or that do not occur uniformly in all Haggadah texts; also to indicate passages recited on the Sabbath or at the close of the Sabbath. The introduction, commentary, and explanatory notes are largely based on the extensive treatment of the subject in E. D. Goldschmidt's *Die Pessach Haggadah*, Berlin 1937, and *Seder Haggadah shel Pesah*, Jerusalem 1947, both published by Schocken. Biblical passages are quoted in the translation issued by the Jewish Publication Society of America, Philadelphia 1916.

For the second revised edition (1969), a section of Readings in Preparation for the Passover was added (pp. vii–xxii). The Introduction and the text of the Haggadah are to be found at the opposite part of the book, starting on pp. 5 and 16, respectively.

For the third revised edition a section of Readings in memory of the Holocaust was added in response to the custom developing in recent years to devote a part of the Seder celebration to the memory of the Holocaust. (The heroic uprising in the Warsaw Ghetto took place on Passover 1943.)

This new expanded edition includes illustrations from the *haggadot* of many lands, reproduced here courtesy of the Library of the Jewish Theological Seminary of America (JTSAL) and Harvard College Library (Harvard). Illustrations not otherwise noted are from the Prague Haggadah of 1526.

READINGS IN PREPARATION FOR THE PASSOVER

THE SEDER CEREMONY
From The Mishnah

On the eve of Passover, when the late afternoon approaches,[1] a man must eat naught until nightfall. Even the poorest in Israel must not eat unless he sits down to table, and they must not give them less than four cups of wine to drink even if it is from the [Paupers'] Dish.[2]

After they have mixed him[3] his first cup, the School of Shammai say: He says the benediction first over the [holy] day and then the benediction over the wine. And the School of Hillel say: He says the benediction first over the wine and then the benediction over the day.

When [food] is brought before him he eats it seasoned with lettuce, until he is come to the bread condiment [the bitter herbs]; they bring before him unleavened bread and lettuce, and the *haroseth*,[4] although *haroseth* is not a religious obligation. Rabbi Eliezer ben Rabbi Zadok says: It is a religious obligation. And in the Holy City they used to bring before him the complete Passover-offering.

They then mix him the second cup. And here the son asks his father (and if the son has not enough understanding his father instructs him [how to ask]): "Why is this night different from other nights? For on other nights we eat seasoned food once, but

Mishnah Pesahim X, 1–8. Translation: Herbert Danby, Clarendon Press, Oxford 1933, pp. 150 f.

this night twice; on other nights we eat leavened or unleavened bread, but this night all is unleavened;[5] on other nights we eat flesh roast, stewed, or cooked, but this night all is roast."[6] And according to the understanding of the son his father instructs him. He begins with the disgrace[7] and ends with the glory; and he expounds from "A wandering Aramean was my father" (Deut. 26:5), until he finishes the whole section.

Rabban Gamaliel[8] used to say: Whosoever has not said [the verses[9] concerning] these three things at Passover has not fulfilled his obligation. And these are they: Passover, unleavened bread, and bitter herbs: "Passover"—because God passed over the houses of our fathers in Egypt; "unleavened bread"—because our fathers were redeemed from Egypt; "bitter herbs"—because the Egyptians embittered the lives of our fathers in Egypt.

In every generation a man must so regard himself as if he came forth himself out of Egypt, for it is written: "And thou shalt tell thy son in that day saying, It is because of that which the Lord did for me when I came forth out of Egypt" (Exod. 13:8). Therefore are we bound to give thanks, to praise, to glorify, to honor, to exalt, to extol, and to bless him who wrought all these wonders for our fathers and for us. He brought us out from bondage to freedom, from sorrow to gladness, and from mourning to a Festival day, and from darkness to great light, and from servitude to redemption; so let us say before him the Hallelujah.[10]

How far do they recite [the Hallel]? The School of Shammai say: To "A joyful mother of children"[11] and the School of Hillel say: To "A flintstone into a springing well."[12] And this is concluded with the [benediction recounting] Redemption.

Rabbi Tarfon says: "He that redeemed us and redeemed our fathers from Egypt and brought us to this night to eat therein unleavened bread and bitter herbs." But there is no concluding benediction.

Rabbi Akiba adds: "Therefore, O Lord our God and the God of our fathers, bring us in peace to the other set feasts and festivals which are coming to meet us, while we rejoice in the building-up of Thy city and are joyful in Thy worship; and may we eat

there of the sacrifices and of the Passover-offerings whose blood has reached with acceptance the wall of Thy altar, and let us praise Thee for our redemption and for the ransoming of our soul. Blessed art Thou, O Lord, who hast redeemed Israel!"

After they have mixed for him the third cup he says the benediction over his meal. [Over] a fourth [cup] he completes the "Hallel" and says after it the benediction over song. If he is minded to drink [more] between these cups he may drink; only between the third and the fourth cups he may not drink.

After the Passover meal they should not disperse to join in revelry.[13]

NOTES

[1] About 3 P.M.

[2] A communal institution for the support of the poorest.

[3] This refers to every participant, not only to the poor.

[4] A dish of nuts and fruit pounded together and mixed with vinegar. The bitter herbs were dipped into this to mitigate their bitterness.

[5] Some texts add: "On other nights we eat all other manner of vegetables, but this night bitter herb."

[6] Some texts add: "On other nights we dip but once, but this night twice."

[7] Egyptian slavery and idolatry.

[8] Son (or grandson) of Hillel the Elder.

[9] Exod. 12:27 and 39; 1:14.

[10] This refers to the "Hallel" Psalms, 113–18.

[11] End of Ps. 113.

[12] End of Ps. 114.

[13] Hebrew *afikoman*; see p. 27.

THE PROHIBITION OF LEAVENED FOOD

PHILO OF ALEXANDRIA

Leavened food is forbidden [during Passover] because of the rising which it produces. Here again we have a symbol of the truth, that none as he approaches the altar should be uplifted or puffed up by arrogance; rather gazing on the greatness of God, let him gain a perception of the weakness which belongs to the creature, even though he may be superior to others in prosperity; and having been thus led to the reasonable conclusion, let him reduce the overweening exaltation of his pride by laying low that pestilent enemy, conceit. For if the Creator and Maker of the universe, though needing nothing of all that He has begotten, has regard to your weakness and not to the vastness of His might and sovereignty, makes you a partaker in His gracious power and fills up the deficiencies that belong to your life, how ought you to treat other men, your natural kinsfolk, seedlings from the same elements as yourself, you who brought nothing into the world, not even yourself? For naked you came into the world, worthy sir, and naked will you again depart, and the span of time between your birth and death is a loan to you from God. During this span what can be meet for you to do but to study fellow-feeling and goodwill and equity and humanity and what else belongs to virtue, and to cast away the inequitable, unrighteous, and unforgiving viciousness which turns man, naturally the most civilized of creatures, into a wild and ferocious animal!

Philo, *The Special Laws*, I, 293 ff. Translation: F. H. Colson, Loeb Classical Library, Harvard University Press, Cambridge, Mass. 1937, VII, pp. 403 ff.

JESUS AND THE LAST SUPPER

Solomon Zeitlin

In the entire literature of the Second Commonwealth nothing is recorded of the ritual of the first night of Passover. There are some isolated passages in the Talmud referring to the period of the Second Commonwealth like "So did Hillel when the Temple stood: he would wrap (the meat of the paschal lamb) together with matzot and bitter herbs and ate them together."[1] Josephus likewise makes reference only to the paschal lamb. He relates that the Jews gathered together as a fraternity for the slaughtering of the paschal lamb and he further says that there were never less than ten persons.[2] This corroborates the statement in the tannaitic literature that the paschal lamb was always sacrificed by a company of not less than ten and this only by invitation.[3]

According to the Synoptic gospels Jesus was arrested on the night that the paschal lamb was sacrificed. In the Gospel according to Mark the disciples asked Jesus, "Where wilt thou that we go and prepare that thou mayest eat the pascha."[4] The Gospel further says, "Jesus took bread and blessed and brake it, and gave to them, and said, 'Take, eat; this is my body.' And he took the cup and when he had given thanks he gave it to them and they all drank of it. And he said to them, 'This is my blood of the testament which is shed for many.' . . . and when they had sung a hymn they went out to the Mount of Olives." The same account is given by the Gospel according to Matthew.[5] The Gospel according to Luke relates that on the day of the unleavened bread when the paschal lamb was to be killed, Jesus sent Peter and John to prepare a place where to eat it. This Gospel adds, "And when the hour was come he sat down and the twelve apostles

The Jewish Quarterly Review, XXVIII, No. 4 (April, 1948).

with him. And he said unto them, 'With desire I have desired to eat this paschal lamb with you before I suffer, for I say unto you I will not any more eat thereof until it be fulfilled in the kingdom of God.' . . . And he took bread and gave thanks and brake it and gave unto them saying 'This is my body which is given for you: This do in remembrance of me.' Likewise also the cup after supper saying 'This cup is the testament of my blood which is shed for you.' "

The description of the Last Supper given in the gospels is undoubtedly a record of the Seder of the first night of Passover. The bread which Jesus ate was unleavened bread and the wine that used by the Jews on the first night of Passover. The hymn sung by Jesus and the Apostles after the meal was the Hallel, which is still sung by the Jews on that night.

Mark and Matthew make no mention that Jesus ate the paschal lamb. Luke relates that Jesus said to his Apostles, "With desire I desired to eat the paschal lamb with you." The reason that Mark, Matthew, and Luke did not mention that Jesus ate the paschal lamb was that they held that Jesus himself was the paschal lamb that was to be sacrificed to redeem men. As Justin Martyr said, "And the blood of the pascha, sprinkled on each man's door-posts and lintel, delivered those who were saved in Egypt, when the first-born of the Egyptians were destroyed. For the pascha was Christ who was afterwards sacrificed . . . And as the blood of the Passover saved us who were in Egypt, so also the blood of Christ will deliver from death those who have believed."[6]

According to the Gospel of John the Last Supper was an ordinary meal, since Jesus was crucified on the eve of Passover. Hence the meal which Jesus ate with his disciples on the preceding night could not have been the Passover meal. The Last Supper, according to John, was on Thursday night, the 13th of the month, and Jesus was arrested and crucified the following morning, Friday, the 14th, a day before Passover.[7]

Paul, in his letter to I Corinthians, says that Jesus on the last night took bread, "And when he had given thanks he brake it and said 'Take, eat, this is my body which is broken for you. This do

in remembrance of me.' After the same manner he took the cup when they had supped, saying 'This cup is the new testament of my blood. This do ye as oft as you drink it in remembrance of me.' "[8]

In the early days of Christianity the followers of Jesus gave thanks (*eucharistia*) over the Bread and the Cup in the sacrament mystery.[9] The Eucharist was called by the Church Fathers *sacramenta altaris*[10] and was applied to the sacrament of the Blood and Body of Jesus. Cyprian explained *eucharistia* by the following words: *id est sanctum Domini corpus.*[11]

The term *eucharistia* never occurs in the Septuagint. It appears a few times in the apochryphal literature[12] and has the connotation of thanks. Philo used the term *eucharistia* in a wider sense. In one place he connects the term *eucharistia* with hymns, prayers and sacrifices.[13] In another place he associates it with the offering of thanks to God for the creation of the universe.[14] The term *eucharistia* as used by Philo has more of a spiritual idea than ordinary thanks and had great influence on early Christianity.[15]

The Pagans, not knowing about the mystery (sacrament) of the Eucharist, accused the Christians of devouring the flesh of infants and using their blood in the sacraments. This monstrous libel was transferred later by the Christians against the Jews— that they used human blood in their paschal meal. Thousands upon thousands of Jews were tortured and put to death as the result of this false accusation. It is true that from time to time some popes issued a bull in which they refuted such libels and said that the Jews were prohibited by their religion from using the blood of animals.

The early Christians celebrated the resurrection of Jesus and called it pascha.[16] It was observed at the same time that the Jews observed Passover. Epiphanius said, "So long at least as the first fifteen bishops of Jerusalem (those of Jewish descent) continued, the pascha was celebrated everywhere by all (Christians), or by a great majority of them, according to the lunar computation and method of the Jews."[17]

The bishops sent out epistles, called paschal epistles, to notify the Christians when pascha (Easter) would fall. At the Council

of Nicea, 325 C.E., the Christians were prohibited from celebrating pascha at the time the Jews were celebrating Passover. The Emperor Constantine, who presided over the Council, said, "Let us have nothing in common with the detestable Jewish crowd." However, down to our time, the date of pascha (Easter) has depended on the vernal equinox and never became a fixed date in the Church. It is usually celebrated approximately about the same time the Jews observe Passover, but in exceptional cases on the Sunday after the festival of Purim.

Not only was pascha (Easter) celebrated at the same time as Passover among the Jews, but its origin is very much interwoven with Passover. Even the institution of the Eucharist is really based on the Jewish custom during the Second Commonwealth of giving thanks to God on the first night of Passover for their redemption, over unleavened bread and a cup of wine. The writings of Philo were a further stimulus to the institution of the Eucharist.

NOTES

[1] See p. 57; see also Pes. 115a.

[2] *Jewish Wars*, VI, 423.

[3] Pes. 64b.

[4] 14:12.

[5] 26:17–30.

[6] *Dialogue With Trypho*, 111.

[7] See S. Zeitlin, "The Date of the Crucifixion According to the Fourth Gospel" (and the literature there quoted), *Journal of Biblical Literature*, 1932.

[8] 11:24–25.

[9] *Sacramentum* is a Latin word and could not have any ecclesiastical usage in the Apostolic age. The word used was mystery (*mysterion*), in Colossians 1:27 and in I Timothy 3:6. The Greek *mysterion* is rendered in the Vulgate *sacramentum*.

[10] Augustine, *De Civitate Dei*, X, 6.

[11] *Epist.* XV, 1, *Corpus Scriptorum a Ecclesiasticorum Latinorum*, 111, 2.

[12] II Mac. 1:2; III Mac. 7:16; Si. 37:11; Wis. 18:2. Comp. also Josephus, *Antiquities*, IV, 13.

[13] *De Special Legibus Lib. I* (*De Victimus*).

[14] *Ibid.* 6.

[15] Comp. Irenaeus, *Contra Haereses*, IV, 18. See also Ignatius to the Smyrnaeans, 7.

[16] This name is used in all the Romance languages (French Pâques, Italian

Pasqua). In the New Testament pascha is always rendered Passover in the English version except in Acts 12:4 where it is wrongly translated Easter.

[17] *Panarion Haer.* 70,10. Comp. also Eusebiu̦s, *Eccles. Hist.* V, 23. "For all the ecclesiastical districts of Asia thought it right, as though by more older tradition to observe the feast of the Saviour's pascha (Easter) the fourteenth day of the moon, on which the Jews were commanded to sacrifice the lamb."

MOSES AND THE EXODUS
From The Talmud and Midrash

The Shepherd

"And Moses was keeping the flock of Jethro his father-in-law" (Exod. 3:1).

God tested Moses by means of the flock.

Once, when he was feeding Jethro's flock in the desert, a kid ran off; he followed it until it reached a shady place. There the kid found a pond and started to drink. When Moses had come close, he said: "I did not know that you ran off because you were thirsty; you must be tired." He took it on his shoulders and went.

Whereupon the Holy One, blessed be He, said: "Moses, you have shown to have compassion in tending the flock of a human; I swear, you shall tend my sheep, Israel" (Exodus Rabba II, 3).

Identity

Israel deserved the exodus from Egypt because they did not change their names, did not change their language, did not engage in evil talk, and preserved the purity of their families.

They did not change their names: They came to Egypt as Reuben and Simeon, and as Reuben and Simeon they left Egypt; Reuben did not become Rufus, Judah did not become Julian, Joseph did not become Justus, and Benjamin did not become Alexander (Midrash Cant. Rabba IV, 24).

The Woman

For the sake of the pious women who lived in that generation were the Israelites freed from the Egyptian bondage (Sotah 11b).

Does the Holy One, blessed be He, rejoice in the downfall of the wicked? Is it not written, ". . . as they went out before the army, they said, 'Give thanks to the Lord, for His steadfast love endureth for ever'" (II Chron. 20:21). Why is the phrase "for He is good" [which is a part of the formula] left out in this thanksgiving?

Because the Holy One, blessed be He, does not rejoice in the downfall of the wicked.

Rabbi Johanan said:

"[When the Israelites crossed the Red Sea] the angels wanted to sing a hymn. But the Holy One, blessed be He, said: 'The work of my hand [the Egyptians] are drowning in the sea, and you want to sing hymns?'" (Megillah 10b).

From TALES OF THE HASIDIM

Martin Buber

The Cantonist at the Seder

It is told:

In the Russia of those days, it was common to draft Jewish boys in the army, in which they were forced to serve to their sixtieth year. They were known as "cantonists."

On the eve of Passover, a man whose uniform identified him as a cantonist arrived in Koznitz and asked to be admitted to the holy maggid. When he stood in his presence, he begged to be allowed to participate in the Seder, and the maggid gave his permission.

When, in the course of the rites of the Seder, they came to the words: "The Ceremony of the Passover has been celebrated in due order," the guest asked whether he might sing, and his request was granted. After the closing words of the song: *peduyim lezion berina*, which means, "Redeemed unto Zion with joy," he cried out in Russian: "Podyom!" that is, "Let's go!" The maggid rose and said in a voice filled with jubilation: "We are ready to go to Zion." But the guest had vanished.

Suffering and Prayer

Whenever Rabbi Levi Yitzhak came to that passage in the Haggadah of Passover which deals with the four sons, and in it read about the fourth son, about him who "knows not how to ask," he said: " 'The one who knows not how to ask,' that is myself, Levi Yitzhak of Berditchev. I do not know how to ask you, Lord of the world, and even if I did know, I could not bear to do it. How could I venture to ask you why everything happens as it

Martin Buber, *Tales of the Hasidim: The Early Masters*, Schocken Books, New York 1948, pp. 294, 212.

does, why we are driven from one exile into another, why our foes are allowed to torment us so. But in the Haggadah, the father of him 'who knows not how to ask,' is told: 'It is for you to disclose it to him.' And the Haggadah refers to the Scriptures, in which it is written: 'And thou shalt tell thy son.' And, Lord of the world, am I not your son? I do not beg you to reveal to me the secret of your ways—I could not bear it! But show me one thing; show it to me more clearly and more deeply: show me what this, which is happening at this very moment, means to me, what it demands of me, what you, Lord of the world, are telling me by way of it. Ah, it is not why I suffer that I wish to know, but only whether I suffer for your sake."

THE FEAST OF DELIVERANCE

FRANZ ROSENZWEIG

The welding of people into a people takes place in its deliverance. And so the feast that comes at the beginning of its national history is a feast of deliverance. Because of this, the Sabbath can legitimately be interpreted as a reminder of the exodus from Egypt. For the freedom of the man-servant and the maid-servant which it proclaims is conditioned by the deliverance of the people as a people from the servitude of Egypt. And in every command to respect the freedom of even the man-servant, of even the alien among the people, the law of God renews the awareness of the connection holding between the freedom within the people, a freedom decreed by God, and the freeing of the people from Egyptian servitude, a liberation enacted by God. Like the creation of the world, the creation of the people contains the final goal, the final purpose for which it was effected. So it is that the people have come to feel this feast as the most vivid of the three, including the meaning of the two others.

Among the many meals of the liturgical year, the evening meal of the Passover at which the father of the household gathers together all his family is the meal of meals. It is the only one that from first to last has the character of worship; hence the Seder ("Order") is, from first to last, liturgically regulated. From the very start the word "freedom" sheds its light upon it. The freedom of this meal at which all are equally free is expressed in a number of rites which "distinguish this night from all nights," among them the reclining of the participants on cushions. And even more vividly than in this reminiscence of the reclining of

Der Stern der Erlösung, III, 72 ff. N. N. Glatzer, *Franz Rosenzweig: His Life and Thought*, Schocken Books, New York 1953, pp. 319 ff.

the guests in the symposia of antiquity, this particular freedom expresses itself in the fact that the youngest child is the one to speak, and that what the father says at that table is adapted to this child's personality and his degree of maturity. In contrast to all instruction, which is necessarily autocratic and never on a basis of equality, the sign of a true and free social intercourse is this, that the one who stands—relatively speaking—nearest the periphery of the circle, gives the cue for the level on which the conversation is to be conducted. For this conversation must include him. No one who is there in the flesh shall be excluded in the spirit. The freedom of a society is always the freedom of everyone who belongs to it. Thus this meal is a symbol of the people's vocation for freedom. That this vocation is only a beginning, only the *initial* creation of the people, is shown in another aspect of this prominence of the youngest child. Since this youngest was permitted to speak for himself, the entire ceremony has, after all, to assume the form of instruction. The father of the family speaks, the household listens, and only in the further course of the evening is there more and more common independence until, in the songs of praise and the table songs of the second part of the meal, songs which float between divine mystery and the jesting mood begot by wine, the last shred of autocracy in the order of the meal dissolves into community.

The founding of the people affords a glimpse of its future destinies, but no more than a glimpse. All its further destinies are prefigured in its origin. It is not only today that enemies rise to destroy us; they rose to destroy us in every generation, back to the first, which went out of Egypt, and in every generation God saved us![1] And we should have been content with what he did for us when he delivered us from the servitude of Egypt, but he to whom he alone suffices did not consider it sufficient. He led us to Mount Sinai and on to the place of rest in his sanctuary.[2] The texts read from the Scriptures on the last days of the feast give a survey from the origin on to what is latent in this origin, in this creation of the people: on to revelation and ultimate redemption. The reading of the Song of Songs[3] points to revelation. A distant

view of redemption is afforded by Isaiah's prophecy[4] of the shoot that shall come forth out of the stock of Jesse and smite the land with the rod of his mouth, of the day when the wolf shall dwell with the lamb and the world shall be as full of the knowledge of the Lord as the sea is of water. But the stock shall stand, an ensign for the peoples, and the heathen shall seek it. And this is the deepest meaning of the farewell which those who participate in the evening meal bid one another: Next year in Jerusalem! In every house where the meal is celebrated a cup filled with wine stands ready for the prophet Elijah, the precursor of the shoot from the stock of Jesse, who is forever "turning the hearts of the fathers to their children and the hearts of the children to their fathers,"[5] so that the flow of blood may not cease during the long night of time, and stream on toward a morning to come.

NOTES

[1] A paraphrase of a passage in the Passover Haggadah; see p. 31.

[2] See p. 45.

[3] Customarily done after the conclusion of the Passover Seder.

[4] Isa. 11:1–10, a part of the portion of the Prophets read on the eighth day of Passover.

[5] Mal. 3:24.

READINGS ON THE HOLOCAUST

LET US REMEMBER

the Holocaust that consumed Jewish men, women and children in the days of Hitler, 1933 to 1945.

Let us remember their sacrifice and their heroism, their agony and their faith.

Auschwitz (Oswiecim)—Belzec—Maidanek—Treblinka—Buchenwald—Theresienstadt (Terezin)—Warsaw (Passover 1943)—Vilna—Bergen-Belsen—Dachau—Lvov.

PASSOVER, BERGEN-BELSEN, 1944*

Our Father in heaven, behold it is evident and known to thee that it is our desire to do thy will and to celebrate the festival of Passover by eating matzah and by observing the prohibition of leavened food. But our heart is pained that the enslavement prevents us and we are in danger of our lives. Behold, we are prepared and ready to fulfill thy commandment: "And ye shall live by them and not die by them."

We pray to thee that thou mayest keep us alive and preserve us and redeem us speedily so that we may observe thy statutes and do thy will and serve thee with a perfect heart. Amen.

The Jewish prisoners in the German concentration camp at Bergen-Belsen did not have matzah for the observance of Passover in 1944. Under the circumstances the sages at the camp permitted the eating of leavened bread for which occasion this benediction was composed.

*Language of Faith, A Selection from the Most Expressive Jewish Prayers, gathered and edited by Nahum N. Glatzer, Schocken Books, New York, 1967, p. 216.

NEVER SHALL I FORGET*

Never shall I forget that night, the first night in camp, which has turned my life into one long night, seven times cursed and seven times sealed. Never shall I forget that smoke. Never shall I forget the little faces of the children, whose bodies I saw turned into wreaths of smoke beneath a silent blue sky.

Never shall I forget those flames which consumed my Father forever.

Never shall I forget that nocturnal silence which deprived me, for all eternity, of the desire to live. Never shall I forget those moments which murdered my God and my soul and turned my dreams to dust. Never shall I forget these things, even if I am condemned to live as long as God himself. Never.

*Elie Wiesel, *Night*, Hill and Wang, New York, 1960.

LETTERS FROM THE GHETTO

February, 1941*

Dearest Bronia, my hand trembles, I cannot write. We fare terribly, our moments are numbered. God alone knows if we'll ever see you again. I write and cry, my children despair—one wants so much to stay alive. All of us say good-bye to all of you. I am not in contact with Hania and Hala, so you, my Bronia, write to them and say good-bye from us. We kiss you. Write immediately, perhaps I shall still receive your letter. If you do not hear from me soon, then we are probably no longer alive.

November 16, 1942**

My Dear, Dear Daddy:

It is late, I am very sleepy, but still I must write you a few words. We receive your letters in regular order. We have already written to you several times, but have received no reply as yet. Today we received from you 200 zlotys; they will be very useful to us. Today we had a sweet day—we were given marmalade and candy.

Lolusz! Your birthday is approaching. This is already the fourth time that we shall celebrate it separately, but full of hope and faith that next year God will grant that we all be together. Our own dear Daddy—you must be strong and steadfast and believe, as we do, that the moment of our meeting is close and we will all be together and happy.

My eyes are closing. I can't write anymore. Good night, Loluszec! Don't worry. I hug and kiss you—I'm full of hope. My heart and soul are with you—

Inja

Dear Lolek!

We're all well and wait impatiently for your reply. Many thanks for the greetings from Stera. We don't know about the rest of them. You be well and strong and in good hope—

I kiss you,

— Nusja

*Holocaust Reader, by Lucy S. Dawidowicz, Behrman, New York, 1976, p. 216.
**Anthology of Holocaust Literature, edited by Jacob Glatstein, Jewish Publication Society, Philadelphia, 1969, p. 161. Translated by Max Rosenfeld.

SONGS*

Forced labor produced a new chapter in Yiddish folklore as dozens of songs, often plaintive and lachrymose, some bitter and ironic, were created to discharge the bitter accumulation of woe. Workers from Radom taken to the labor camp at Cieszanów used to lament:

> Work, brothers, work fast,
> If you don't, they'll lash your hide.
> Not many of us will manage to last—
> Before long we'll all have died.

Marching slave-labor brigades in the Libau ghetto used to sing:

> We are the ghetto Jews,
> The loneliest people on earth.
> Everything we had we lost,
> We have nothing left of worth.

To boost morale, the slave-labor brigades in the Kovno ghetto sang:

> We don't weep or grieve
> Even when you beat and lash us,
> But never for a moment believe
> That you will discourage and dash us.

> Jewish brigades,
> With rags for clothes
> March day in, day out
> And bravely bear their woes.

I BELIEVE**

Inscription on the walls of a cellar in Cologne, Germany, where Jews hid from Nazis.

> I believe in the sun even when it is not shining.
> I believe in love even when feeling it not.
> I believe in God even when He is silent.

*The War Against the Jews 1933–1945, by Lucy S. Dawidowicz, Holt, Rinehart and Winston, New York, 1975, pp. 202 f.
**The Judaic Tradition, Edited by Nahum N. Glatzer, Beacon Press, 1972, p. 623.

IF GOD LETS ME LIVE
ANNE FRANK

[Anne Frank was born in Germany in 1929; her family emigrated to Holland in 1933. She wrote her diary *(Anne Frank: Diary of a Young Girl)*, from which the following excerpt is taken, between 1942 and 1944, while in hiding in an attic during the Nazi occupation in Holland. In March 1945 she died in the concentration camp of Bergen-Belsen. Later, her diary was discovered.]

[. . .] We have been pointedly reminded that we are in hiding, that we are Jews in chains, chained to one spot, without any rights, but with a thousand duties. We Jews mustn't show our feelings, must be brave and strong, must accept all inconveniences and not grumble, must do what is within our power and trust in God. Sometime this terrible war will be over. Surely the time will come when we are people again, and not just Jews.

Who has inflicted this upon us? Who has made us Jews different from all other people? Who has allowed us to suffer so terribly up till now? It is God that has made us as we are, but it will be God, too, who will raise us up again. If we bear all this suffering and if there are still Jews left, when it is over, then Jews, instead of being doomed, will be held up as an example. Who knows, it might even be our religion from which the world and all peoples learn good, and for that reason and that reason only do we have to suffer now. We can never become just Netherlanders, or just English, or representatives of any country for that matter, we will always remain Jews, but we want to, too. . . .

If God lets me live, I shall attain more than Mummy ever has done, I shall not remain insignificant, I shall work in the world and for mankind!

And now I know that first and foremost I shall require courage and cheerfulness!

Yours, Anne

Title page of a haggadah composed by survivors shortly after World War II.
Landsberg, Germany, 1947 (HARVARD).

"In every generation, each person should regard himself as if
he came out from Egypt." Page from a haggadah printed in Munich after the Holocaust.
Munich, Germany, 1948 (HARVARD).

GUIDE TO NAMES, WORKS, AND TERMS

ABRAVANEL, ISAAC: b. Lisbon, 1437; d. Venice, 1508. Statesman, biblical commentator, philosophical writer. Also wrote a commentary on the Passover Haggadah.

AKIBA: leading Palestinian teacher (Tanna) of the 2nd cent. C. E.

AMORA: title of sages who lived at the time of the Gemara (see Talmud).

AMRAM: Gaon (q. v.) in Sura, Babylonia; 9th cent. His most important work is his Order of Prayer (Seder Rav Amram).

AVUDRAHAM: David ben Joseph Avudraham of Seville. Wrote (1370) a commentary on the prayers (Sefer Avudraham, first printed in 1489).

BANETH, EDUARD: 1855–1930; professor of Talmud at the Hoschschule für die Wissenschaft des Judentums in Berlin.

BARAITA: a tradition of the Tannaim which is not contained in the Mishnah.

BAR KOKHBA: leader of the rebellion of the Jews against Emperor Hadrian (132–135 C. E.).

DESTRUCTION: of the First Temple, 586 B. C. E.; of the Second, 70 C. E.

EMDEN, JACOB: talmudist in Altona and Emden, Germany, 18th cent.

EXODUS RABBAH: midrash (q. v.) on the Book of Exodus.

FINKELSTEIN, LOUIS: contemporary American-Jewish scholar; Chancellor, Jewish Theological Seminary of America.

GAMALIEL (THE ELDER): a grandson of Hillel; leading sage in the time before the destruction of the Second Temple; grandfather of Gamaliel the Second.

GAMALIEL (THE SECOND): leading Palestinian sage after the destruction of the Second Temple.

GAON: title of the heads of the Babylonian academies from 6th to 11th cent.

GAON OF VILNA: Rabbi Elijah, leading talmudic authority of the 18th cent.

GENIZAH: "hiding place," repository of sacred books no longer used; particularly applied to the Ezra Synagogue in Cairo, built in the 7th cent., rediscovered end of the 19th cent. The texts and fragments found in the Genizah greatly enriched Jewish literature.

HEIDENHEIM, WOLF: b. 1757, Heidenheim, Germany; d. 1832, Rödelheim, Germany. Hebrew grammarian; editor of classical liturgic texts.

HILLEL: outstanding sage in Jerusalem in the 1st cent. B. C. E.; founder

of the school called after him (House of Hillel, Bet Hillel); ancestor of the patriarchs who headed Palestinian Jewry till the 5th cent. The House of Hillel stood in opposition to the House of Shammai.

HIRSCH, S. R.: rabbi in Frankfort on the Main, 19th cent.; founder of neo-orthodoxy. Author of biblical commentaries and of *Horeb*, a book of Jewish theology.

HORAYOT: talmudic tractate.

JABNEH (or YAVNEH): seat of the Sanhedrin after the destruction of Jerusalem and the Second Temple.

JOSE: Palestinian teacher (Tanna) of the 2nd cent. C. E.

JOSEPH TOV ELEM (BONFILS): commentator on Bible and Talmud; liturgical poet; France, 11th cent.

JUBILEES, BOOK OF: apocryphal book on Genesis and Exodus, written in the period of the Second Temple.

KALIR: Eleazar Kalir, great liturgical poet of the early Middle Ages.

LURIA, ISAAC: b. Jerusalem, 1534; d. Safed, Palestine, 1572. Leader of kabbalistic movement of Safed.

MAHARAL: Loev Judah ben Bezalel of Prague, 16th cent.; talmudist and Jewish thinker.

MAHARIL: Jacob ben Moses ha-Levi, b. about 1355 in Mainz, Germany; d. 1427 in Worms, Germany. Rabbi in Mainz; authority on liturgy and synagogue customs.

MAHZOR ROMA: order of prayer according to the Italian ritual; first printing Soncino, Italy, 1485–86.

MAHZOR ROMANIA: order of prayer according to the original custom of the Balkan countries; earliest extant edition, Venice 1524.

MAHZOR VITRY: order of prayer and liturgical work compiled by Simhah ben Samuel of Vitry, France, a disciple of Rashi (q. v.); 11th cent.

MAIMONIDES: Moses ben Maimon, b. 1135, Cordova; d. 1204, Cairo. Principal works: Mishneh Torah, first systematic code of Jewish law and religion; Moreh Nevukhim (Guide to the Perplexed), comprehensive theological work. (The laws regarding Passover are contained in the section Hametz u-Matzah of the Mishneh Torah.)

MASORAH: the work of preserving the traditional text of the Scriptures. A biblical text not in accordance with the Masorah is, e. g., the one which was the basis of the Septuagint translation.

MEGILLAH: talmudic tractate.

MEKHILTA: tannaitic midrash on Exod. (quoted according to the passage in Exod.).

MIDRASH: exegesis of Scriptures, especially of non-legal portions, compiled in the talmudic period and in following centuries. Midrashic collections include e. g., Mekhilta, Sifra, Sifre; Midrash Rabbah (q. v.),

Midrash Tanhuma, Pesikta Rabbati, Pesikta de Rav Kahana, Tanna debe Eliyahu.

MIDRASH RABBAH: midrash (q. v.) on the Pentateuch and the Five Scrolls (quoted according to chapter and paragraph).

MIDRASH TEHILLIM: midrash on Psalms (quoted according to folio in the S. Buber edition).

MISHNAH: code of law; the earliest part of the Talmud; based on older collections of laws; completed by the end of the 2nd cent. c. e. (quoted according to chapter and paragraph).

NISAN: Hebrew month (March-April). The Fourteenth of Nisan: eve of Passover; the fifteenth and sixteenth: the first and second days of Passover.

PESAHIM: talmudic tractate dealing with Passover laws and the laws relating to the paschal lamb. See Talmud.

PESIKTA DE RAV KAHANA: a midrashic work (quoted according to chapter).

PESIKTA RABBATI: a midrashic work (quoted according to chapter).

PHILO: Jewish philosopher of the Hellenistic period, b. ca. 20 B. C. E.; lived in Alexandria, Egypt.

PIRKE DE RABBI ELIEZER: a midrashic work (quoted according to chapter).

RASHI: Solomon ben Isaac, Troyes, France, 11th cent. Authoritative commentator on Bible and Babylonian Talmud.

RAV: talmudic master of the 3rd cent.; Babylonia.

ROSH HA-SHANAH: talmudic tractate.

SAADIA: Gaon (q. v.) in Sura, Babylonia; 9th–10th cent. Philosopher and talmudic authority. He is also compiler of an Order of Prayer (Siddur).

SAMUEL: talmudic master of the 3rd cent.; Babylonia.

SANHEDRIN: (synhedrion), highest court of Jewish law; assembly of seventy-one sages which interpreted the law. Also name of a talmudic tractate.

SEPTUAGINT: Greek translation of the Bible; the Pentateuch was translated about 250 B. C. E.

SHAMMAI: see Hillel.

SIFRE: tannaitic midrash to Num. and Deut. (quoted according to book and paragraph in the M. Friedmann edition).

SOTAH: talmudic tractate.

TAANIT: talmudic tractate.

TALMUD: consists of (1) Mishnah (q. v.); (2) Gemara ("completion"), discussion of Mishnah in academies of Palestine (Talmud Yerushalmi or Palestinian Talmud, compiled ca. end 4th cent.) and of Babylonia (Talmud Babli or Babylonian Talmud, compiled ca. end 5th cent.). The Talmud Yerushalmi (Yer.) is quoted according to the folio and

column of the Krotoschin edition. A tractate quoted without qualification refers to the Babylonian Talmud. It is quoted according to the folio and page of the current editions.

TANHUMA: a midrash on the Pentateuch (quoted according to biblical book and folio in the S. Buber edition).

TANNA DEBE ELIYAHU: a midrashic work.

TANNAIM: sages and masters who lived before the completion of the Mishnah (q. v.). Singular: Tanna.

TOSEFTA: ("supplement"): collection of tannaitic traditions, closely related to the Mishnah (quoted according to tractate, chapter and paragraph).

YALKUT SHIMEONI: a midrashic compilation on the Bible; quoted according to book and paragraph.

YANNAI: one of the earliest liturgical poets; Palestine, 6th cent.

YAVNEH: see Jabneh.

YEMENITE RITUAL: order of prayer of the Jews of Yemen, strongly influenced by Maimonides (q. v.).

YOHANAN (or JOHANAN): talmudic master of the 3rd cent., Palestine.

YOMA: talmudic tractate.

ZEITLIN, SOLOMON: contemporary American-Jewish scholar; professor of rabbinical literature at Dropsie College.

ZUNZ, LEOPOLD: b. 1794, Detmold, Germany; d. 1886, Berlin. Jewish scholar; founder of the "Wissenschaft des Judentums."

הגדה של פסח

THE PASSOVER HAGGADAH

A baroque title page depicting Moses and Aaron, above, and the Sacrifice of Isaac, below. Sulzbach, Bavaria, 1711 (JTSAL).

הגדה של פסח

THE PASSOVER HAGGADAH

WITH HEBREW AND ENGLISH
TRANSLATION ON FACING PAGES

Introduction and Commentary
Based on the Studies of E. D. Goldschmidt

Edited by Nahum N. Glatzer

Including Readings on the Holocaust
With Illustrations from the Earliest Printed Haggadot

SCHOCKEN BOOKS · NEW YORK

Library of Congress Cataloging in Publication Data
Jews. Liturgy and ritual.
The Passover Haggadah.
1. Jews. Liturgy and ritual. Haggadah—Commentaries.
I. Glatzer, Nahum Norbert, 1903—   II. Goldschmidt,
Ernst Daniel.   III. Sloan, Jacob.   IV. Title.
BM675.P4Z555258   1979   296.4'37   79-401
ISBN 0-805-20880-1

Manufactured in the United States of America

Grateful acknowledgment is made to the following for permission to reprint
previously published material:

Excerpt from *Anne Frank: The Diary of a Young Girl.* Copyright 1952 by Otto
Frank. Reprinted by permission of Doubleday & Company, Inc.

Excerpt from Jacob Glatstein, ed., *Anthology of Holocaust Literature* copyrighted and reprinted courtesy of The Jewish Publication Society of America.

A selection from *The Tiger Beneath the Skin* by Zvi Kolitz. Copyright 1947 by
Creative Age Press, Inc. (now a division of Farrar, Straus & Giroux, Inc.).
Copyright renewed 1974 by Zvi Kolitz. Reprinted with the permission of
Farrar, Straus & Giroux, Inc.

A selection from *Night* by Elie Wiesel. Translated from the French by Stella
Rodway. Copyright © 1958 by Les Editions de Minuit. English translation
copyright © 1960 by MacGibbon & Kee. Reprinted with the permission of
Hill & Wang, a division of Farrar, Straus & Giroux, Inc.

INTRODUCTION

1. PASSOVER

For thousands of years the people of Israel have not forgotten that their ancestors were slaves in the land of Egypt. The passage from slavery into freedom became the chief event of Israelite history. Classical Hebrew writings lay stress on the fact that the external liberation was not an end in itself but the necessary precondition for the receiving of the Law on Mount Sinai — the sublime climax of Israel's liberation which took place thirty-two centuries ago.

"In every generation let each man look on himself as if *he* came forth out of Egypt." This tenet strove to make the Exodus from serfdom into freedom a living personal experience. It was in this spirit that the story of the liberation was told and handed down from father to son, the son in turn growing up in the knowledge that he would have to tell "his" story to his children. The Seder became the symbol of the bond between the individual and the family, and between these two and the people, all united in the telling of the old but ever renewed story.

2. THE PASSOVER HAGGADAH AND THE SEDER

The term Passover Haggadah (*Haggadah shel Pesah*) in its literal sense means the narration of the Exodus story as recited at the Seder service. The Seder (Aramaic for the Hebrew *Erekh*, meaning "order" of service) is the festival meal and home service on the first and second night of Passover. In its wider sense the term Passover Haggadah refers to the manual for the Seder; this manual is comprised of selections from the Holy Scriptures, their expositions in talmudic and midrashic literature, prayers and benedictions, legends and hymns, and a guide for the ritual of the ceremony.

The custom of telling the story of the deliverance from Egypt

5

goes back to the scriptural command: "And thou shalt tell thy son in that day, saying: It is because of that which the Lord did to me when I came forth out of Egypt" (Exod. 13:8).

The Mishnah contains the order of the Haggadah in synoptic form (Tractate Pesahim, Chap. X). The earliest full version is preserved in the *Order of Prayer of Rav Saadia Gaon* (10th cent.), it differs somewhat from our present Haggadah, particularly at the beginning. The Haggadah in the *Mahzor Vitry* (11th cent.), closely corresponds to the Haggadah of today, except that it lacks a few liturgical poems that have been appended to the end of the Seder.

3. THE PASSOVER SEDER AND THE DINNER OF ANTIQUITY

A general acquaintance with the Dinner of antiquity will be helpful for an understanding of the Seder ritual.

The Dinner of Greek and Roman antiquity usually began with wine (*yayin shelifne ha-mazon*) and hors d'oeuvre (*gustus*), which the diners on ceremonious occasions frequently took while seated (*yoshevin*) in the antechamber. They then turned to the actual meal, eaten while reclining on pillows. The main course, bread with meat or fish, was taken as a rule with wine (*yayin shebetokh ha-mazon*). A dessert of fruit or other delicacies concluded the meal. Grace was followed by a long bout of drinking (*yayin shelahar ha-mazon*).

The same, in substance, was the order of the Passover meal. The first cup, for "the sanctification of the day," was followed by the hors d'oeuvres which consisted frequently of raw vegetables, lettuce (*hazeret, lactuca*) being a favorite. Meat was the main dish; in the period of the Temple the paschal lamb was roasted and served with unleavened bread and bitter herbs (Exod. 12:8). The second cup of wine accompanied the main dish.

The text of the Mishnah leaves no doubt that immediately after the hors d'oeuvres — the first dipping of raw vegetables — the main dish was served. At this point the child would express his amazement at the strange procedure and would ask the customary Questions. The answer, which traditionally had to begin with the

6

story of the "humiliation" of the Israelites and to end with one of "glory," consisted of an exposition of Deutoronomy 26:5–9 that began at a critical point in Jewish history and climactically concluded with the entrance into the Land of Israel and the building of the Temple. The meal was followed by two cups, one as usual after Grace, the other after the chanting of Psalms 113–118 (*Hallel*).

In the course of the centuries, the ritual of the Seder has undergone only one decisive change: the Questions and the Haggadah recital were advanced to a position before the meal. The reason for this change, which already makes its appearance in the Talmud, was probably a fear lest the recital of the Haggadah suffer after the meal and the drinking of wine. This change, however, caused the loss of a direct immediate relation between the Questions and the ritual of the meal.

4. The Arrangement of the Seder Table

The table is festively bedecked and every celebrant is provided with a winecup. The Seder plate is placed before the master of the Seder ceremony. The following are conveniently disposed on the plate:

1. Three wafers of unleavened bread (*matzot*), separated by cloths which make it possible to cover and uncover the wafers whenever necessary during the course of the Seder. *Matzah shemurah* (literally, "guarded matzah"— ritually supervised from the planting of the grain through the baking of the wafer) is preferred. The three wafers of unleavened bread are a reference and contrast to the two loaves of leavened bread over which the Benediction on Bread is recited on Sabbaths and festivals other than Passover.

2. *Maror*, or bitter herbs, for which various salads are satisfactory. It is customary to use lettuce, endives, or horseradish. In some countries two kinds of bitter herbs are employed: one is eaten in fulfilment of the commandment to eat a bitter herb during the Seder, the other reserved for the combination of unleavened bread and bitter herbs that is eaten before the meal.

3. *Haroset*. In antiquity this pap made of crushed fruit, mostly apples, nuts, and almonds, to which ginger or cinnamon and wine were added, was the common raw vegetable sauce.

4. The "two dishes" (*shene tavshilin*). One of the dishes represents symbolically the paschal lamb, the other commemorates the festival offering made by the pilgrims in Jerusalem on the holiday (*hagigah*). It is customary to use a roasted shankbone (*zeroa*) with a little meat on it for the first of the "two dishes," and a hard-boiled egg for the second. They are both purely commemorative and not intended to be eaten. Nevertheless, they must be made edible.

5. *Karpas*, the first vegetable to be dipped in the salt water. Celery or parsley are generally preferred, though other vegetables, such as radishes and potatoes, can also be used.

6. A dish of salted water or vinegar in which to dip the *karpas*.

Everyone, "even the poorest man in Israel," is obliged to partake of four cups of wine during the Seder. Red wine, considered superior to the other varieties, is to be preferred. There were times, however, when red wine was deliberately avoided, for fear of the ritual blood accusation that was made against the Jews in the Middle Ages (and occasionally later) during Passover time.

The meaning and purpose of the Seder foods is self-evident. In addition, a symbolic significance was attached to them. Rabban Gamaliel (1st cent.) interprets the bitter herbs as symbolic of the bitter hardships endured by the Jews in Egypt, the unleavened bread the suddenness of their redemption (Mishnah Pesahim X.9). Yerushalmi Pesahim 29c gives this explanation for the use of lettuce: "Just as lettuce at first tastes sweet and then bitter, so did the Egyptians treat our ancestors when they were in Egypt. At first they settled them in the best part of the land . . . but later they embittered their lives."

Calling the unleavened bread the "bread of poverty" furnished an occasion of many talmudic explanations of that symbol. Pesahim

115b: "Samuel said: The Bread of Affliction (*oni*) is so called because many words are spoken (*onin*) about it." The later Kabbalists called the three matzot, *kohen* (priest), *levi* (levite), and *yisrael* (Israelite), together constituting a symbol for the entire Jewish community.

Later interpretations make the shankbone (*zeroa*) a symbol of God's "mighty arm," and the egg an allusion to his loving-kindness. Some have interpreted the egg as a symbol of mourning for the destruction of the Temple.

The *haroset* was interpreted as a symbol of the clay out of which the Israelites made bricks for Pharaoh.

Many explanations have been given for the four cups of wine; the most popular one holds that they commemorate the four verbs referring to the act of redemption in the biblical passage where God promises to save the Israelites (Exod. 6:6–7). "How do we know that four cups are required? Rabbi Yohanan said in the name of Rabbi Benayah that they correspond to the four redemptions. . . . Rabbi Levi said they correspond to the four Empires, and the Rabbis said that they correspond to the four cups of wrath that God shall one day give the heathen to drink . . . ." (Yerushalmi Pesahim 37b.)

It is customary to arrange the various items on the Seder platter in the order of their use: first the *karpas* and salt water, then the bitter herbs and *haroset*, and finally the egg and shankbone.

Following the ancient usage, the meal as a whole, and particularly the unleavened bread and the wine, is eaten in a reclining position. It is customary to provide pillows at the Seder, especially for the master of the ceremony.

5. THE COURSE OF THE SEDER

The complete structure of the Seder ritual early prompted the use of rhymes and mnemonic devices to guide the celebrants through the service. The favorite mnemonic composition reads:

Kaddesh u-rehatz, karpas yahatz, maggid rahatz, motzi matzah;
maror korekh, shulkhan orekh, tzafun barekh, hallel nirtzah.

Kaddesh: sanctify (benediction on wine)
u-rehatz: and wash the hands
karpas: dip greens in salt water
yahatz: divide the middle matzah
maggid: he narrates the Haggadah
rahatz: washing of the hands
motzi: benediction on bread
matzah: benediction on unleavened bread
maror: bitter herbs
korekh: he combines matzah with bitter herbs
shulkhan orekh: he sets the table
tzafun: the concealed (afikoman) is eaten
barekh: recite the grace
hallel: recite the Hallel psalms
nirtzah: closing songs.

It is surprising that the last three cups of wine are not mentioned in this mnemonic; apparently their place in the service was considered self-evident.

6. Some Seder Customs

In many countries it is customary for the master of the Seder to wear a white overgarment, known as the *kittel.* Many reasons have been given for the wearing of the *kittel,* the most plausible one being that it is a holiday dress and thus particularly suited for the Seder. According to the Haggahot Maimoniot (Hilkhot Shabbat 30,2), the *kittel* serves a dual purpose: on the one hand it represents the usual festive dress, and on the other it is a sobering reminder of the burial shroud. The Maharal believed that the *kittel* commemorates the service of the High Priest in the ancient Temple.

In some places it is customary for the master of the Seder, before setting aside the *afikoman* which had been wrapped in a cloth, to lay it on his shoulder, take a few steps, and recite the following: "This is in memory of our forefathers, who left Egypt bearing their kneading troughs wrapped in their clothes upon their shoulders." This custom has not gained wide acceptance.

The custom of raising the cup while reciting the prayer begin-

ning, "And it is this promise" (*vehi sheamdah*) is missing from the older editions of the Haggadah and the books that deal with the Ashkenazic ritual. This practice originated with Rabbi Isaac Luria (16th cent.), and has since been accepted into many rituals.

According to the commentators on the Haggadah, the custom of opening the door before reciting the prayer beginning, "Pour out thy wrath" (*shefokh hamatekha*), is derived from the belief that there is no need to keep the door closed during the "night of vigil" commemorating the Exodus. Although the custom of keeping the door open on that night is very ancient, its association with Elijah and the messianic redemption is comparatively late. It is also reasonable to assume that during periods when the Jews were being persecuted, the door was opened in order to make certain that no foe or informer was lying in wait outside.

Connected with the above is the practice of setting (in the center of the table) a cup in honor of Elijah, the harbinger of messianic deliverance, who is believed to visit the homes on the night of the Seder. Elijah's cup is not mentioned in many Haggadah editions. It has been plausibly linked with the dispute as to whether four cups of wine or five should be taken. Since no satisfactory decision was reached, as a compromise a fifth cup is poured out but is not drunk. According to an ancient folk belief Elijah will appear shortly before the coming of the Messiah and resolve all doubts and disputes. It is possible that for this reason the fifth cup became known as the Cup of Elijah and a likely subject for the exercise of the folk imagination.

In keeping with a popular folkway, the children "steal" the *afikoman* and refuse to return it to the master of the Seder (usually the father of the family) until he promises them some reward. Obviously, the "stealing" of the *afikoman* was intended to encourage the children to stay awake until the end of the service.

7. THE HAGGADAH AS A BOOK

Originally the Haggadah made up a section within the prayer book; later it was made into a separate book. As such it can be traced back to thirteenth-century Spain. In the same period illus-

trated Haggadahs appear. A Haggadah manuscript in the Mocatta Library in London (13th cent.) pictures the matzah and bitter herbs and, appended to the text, has a series of vividly colored full-page illustrations of Genesis and Exodus which had been executed for illuminated Bibles.

Later (in the 14th cent.) the Exodus stories directly related to the Haggadah were given preference and were woven in different ways into the text of the Haggadah itself. The most important Haggadot of this pattern are the British Museum manuscripts and the Haggadah of Sarajevo. An interesting incunabulum, containing the Haggadah and other liturgical texts originated in Spain before 1480 (Schocken Collection, Jerusalem).

In distinction from the Spanish type, the Central European (German, French, Italian) Haggadah places its illustrations in the margin and along the lower borders of the page. The pictures, which are quite often partially colored drawings of a lively nature, are concerned with biblical personages and the Exodus from Egypt, with Jewish legends and with Passover rites and symbols; they also illustrate phrases occurring in the Haggadah. Some manuscripts have illustrations of a lighter kind (for instance, the master of the Seder explaining the meaning of the bitter herbs while pointing at his wife). Among the outstanding Ashkenazic Haggadot are the manuscript in the Bibliothèque Nationale in Paris and the Nuremberg Haggadah (both 15th cent.).

The Darmstadt manuscript (early 15th cent.) constitutes a connecting link between both groups of Haggadot; its miniatures are among the most beautiful of the Haggadah illustrations.

The invention of printing did not mark the end of handwritten and illustrated Haggadot; a number of such Haggadot dating from the sixteenth, seventeenth, and eighteenth centuries have been preserved.

The prayer book, printed in 1485 by Joshua Solomon Soncino, also included a Passover Haggadah. The first important separate edition of the Haggadah was done in Prague in 1526 by Gershon ben Solomon ha-Kohen; it was illustrated by quaint woodcuts which breathe the late medieval atmosphere. Some of these woodcuts

are reproduced in the present Haggadah. The Prague Haggadah served as a prototype for the oldest Italian editions with woodcuts (Mantua 1560 and 1568). The Mantua Haggadah was imitated in a Venice imprint (early 17th cent.), which in turn was imitated by most of the later Sephardic editions.

A new chapter in the history of Haggadah printing began with the edition of 1695 in Amsterdam, where much of Jewish publishing was concentrated after Venice ceased to be the center of printing. The illustrations to the Amsterdam Haggadah — copper engravings — served as an example for most of the subsequent Ashkenazic editions, well into the nineteenth century when new trends and techniques appeared. All in all there have been over a thousand different editions of the Haggadah, among which there were more than two hundred illustrated ones.

8. Haggadah Commentaries

The exegesis of the Haggadah has busied Jewish scholars since the eleventh century. Most of the commentaries are homiletic, sometimes mystical, in character. At first the exegesis of the Haggadah stayed close to the text; later the exegetical discourse became an end in itself and only a tenuous connection with the text was maintained.

There are more than three hundred printed commentaries on the Haggadah. In Mahzor Vitry and Sefer ha-Orah, two works composed by disciples of Rashi (11th cent.), there are sections which are designated *perush ha-haggadah*, Haggadah commentary.

Some of the more outstanding commentators are:

The "pseudo Rashbam" (Samuel ben Meir, a grandson of Rashi, of Rameru, 11th–12th cent.). Yomtov ben Abraham (called Ritba; Spain, 13th–14th cent.). Simeon ben Tzemah Duran (called Rashbatz; Mallorca and Algiers, 14th–15th cent.). Isaac ben Judah Abravanel (Lisbon and Venice, 15th–16th cent.; first edition of his commentary, Constantinople, 1505). Joseph Shalit Ashkenazi (first edition, 1550). Moses Pesante (first edition, 1569). Zedekiah de Pietosi (author of *Shibbole ha-Leket*, 1546). The author of *Kol Bo*.

David ben Joseph Avudraham (Seville, 14th cent.; author of *Sefer Avudraham*; first edition, 1489), particularly noteworthy for his contribution toward an understanding of the Haggadah text. Eliezer Ashkenazi (Cremona, Naxos, and Cracow, 16th cent.; author of *Maase Adonai*; first edition, 1583). Loev Judah ben Bezalel (called the Maharal of Prague, 16th cent.; author of *Gevurat Hashem*; first edition in 1582). Isaiah Horovitz (Prague and Safed, 16th–17th cent.). Jacob Zevi Emden (called Yaabetz; Altona, 18th cent.). Elijah the Gaon of Vilna (called Hagra; 18th cent.). Jacob ben Jacob Moses of Lissa (18th–19th cent.). Hayyim Joseph David Azulai (Hebron and Livorno, 18th–19th cent.; author of *Simhat ha-Regel*).

In recent years a number of commentaries of importance have appeared, including H. Edelmann's commentary (Koenigsberg 1845 and Danzig 1845); A. L. Landshuth's introduction, *Maggid Mereshit*, Berlin 1856; that of D. Cassel, Berlin 1888; M. Friedmann's *Meir Ayyin al Hahaggadah shel Pesah*, Vienna 1895; I. D. Eisenstein's *Otzar Perushim Ve-tziyurim al Haggadah shel Pesah*, New York 1920; the editions of Shevach Knebel, Vienna 1923; Kaplan, Warsaw 1924; Cecil Roth, Soncino Press, London 1934.

Special attention merit *Der Sederabend*, by Eduard Baneth, Berlin 1904; *Ein Vortrag über das Ritual des Pessachabends*, by Israel Lewy, Breslau 1904; Louis Finkelstein's articles on "Pre-Maccabean Documents in the Passover Haggadah" in the *Harvard Theological Review* (XXXI and XXXVI); Solomon Zeitlin's "The Liturgy of the First Night of Passover" in *Jewish Quarterly Review* (XXXVIII); "Von der Holbeinbibel zur Amsterdamer Haggadah" (on Haggadah illustrations), by Rahel Wischnitzer-Bernstein in *Monatsschrift für Geschichte und Wissenschaft des Judentums*, vol. 75 (1931); *Passover: Its History and Traditions*, by Theodor H. Gaster, New York 1949. Three important articles on the Haggadah are included in *Studies in Jewish History and Booklore*, by Alexander Marx, New York 1944.

For a bibliography see A. Yaari, *Bibliography of the Passover Haggadah*, Jerusalem 1960, and the *Addenda*, ed. Th. Wiener, *Studies in Bibliography and Booklore*, vol. VII (1965). See also E.

D. Goldschmidt, *The Passover Haggadah, Its Sources and History*, Jerusalem 1960, and Philip Goodman, *The Passover Anthology*, Philadelphia 1961.

די זוילכן דין חמץ אין אלי פיקן אונ'שפאלטן • אונ' בו מורנבם בוור ברענן טונן זי עם ביהאלטן :

Searching for the leaven. Venice, Italy, 1609 (JTSAL).

15

Milling wheat and baking matzoh.
Leghorn, Italy, 1878 (JTSAL).

האר אלמרא קעדא תבّٔסל فّל' פوخّאر ומאעون נחש

האר אלמרא קעדא תפّתש فّّر חמץ מן אסנאדק וקבלתא אסנדוק

האר אלמרא خّעדא תבّٔסל فّל' כّودרא מתע פסח כּאب תכולוا

האר אלמרא קעדא תגרבל فّטעאם כّאס תעמّל אלفّטאיّיר

Women preparing for Passover. Captions are in Judeo-Arabic for the Jews of Tunis, for whom this haggadah was printed. Leghorn, Italy, 1878 (JTSAL).

The first cup of wine is poured, and the master of the Seder recites the Sanctification (*kiddush*), the words in brackets being added on the Sabbath.

וַיְהִי־עֶרֶב וַיְהִי־בֹקֶר

יוֹם הַשִּׁשִׁי. וַיְכֻלּוּ הַשָּׁמַיִם וְהָאָרֶץ וְכָל־צְבָאָם: וַיְכַל אֱלֹהִים בַּיּוֹם הַשְּׁבִיעִי מְלַאכְתּוֹ אֲשֶׁר עָשָׂה. וַיִּשְׁבֹּת בַּיּוֹם הַשְּׁבִיעִי מִכָּל־מְלַאכְתּוֹ אֲשֶׁר עָשָׂה: וַיְבָרֶךְ אֱלֹהִים אֶת־יוֹם הַשְּׁבִיעִי וַיְקַדֵּשׁ אֹתוֹ כִּי בוֹ שָׁבַת מִכָּל־מְלַאכְתּוֹ אֲשֶׁר בָּרָא אֱלֹהִים לַעֲשׂוֹת:]

בָּרוּךְ אַתָּה יְיָ אֱלֹהֵינוּ מֶלֶךְ הָעוֹלָם. בּוֹרֵא פְּרִי הַגָּפֶן:

בָּרוּךְ אַתָּה יְיָ אֱלֹהֵינוּ מֶלֶךְ הָעוֹלָם. אֲשֶׁר בָּחַר בָּנוּ מִכָּל־עָם. וְרוֹמְמָנוּ מִכָּל־לָשׁוֹן. וְקִדְּשָׁנוּ בְּמִצְוֹתָיו. וַתִּתֶּן־לָנוּ יְיָ אֱלֹהֵינוּ בְּאַהֲבָה וְשַׁבָּתוֹת לִמְנוּחָה וּ]מוֹעֲדִים לְשִׂמְחָה חַגִּים וּזְמַנִּים לְשָׂשׂוֹן. אֶת־יוֹם וְהַשַּׁבָּת הַזֶּה

A hare-hunting scene is frequently used to remind the reader of the correct order of the blessings. The German *Jag den Has* recalls the Hebrew mnemonic YaKNeHaZ. The mnemonic stands for *ya*yin (wine), *k*iddush (sanctification), *ne*r (light), *hav*dalah (separation), and *z*eman (time).

The first cup of wine is poured, and the master of the Seder
recites the Sanctification (*kiddush*), the words in brackets being
added on the Sabbath.

THE KIDDUSH

["And there was evening and there was morning, the sixth day.

And the heaven and the earth were finished, and all the host of
them. And on the seventh day God finished His work which He
had made; and He rested on the seventh day from all His work
which He had made. And God blessed the seventh day, and hallowed it; because that in it He rested from all His work which
God in creating had made" (Gen. 1:31; 2:1–3).]

Blessed art thou, O Lord our God, creator of the fruit of the vine.

Blessed art thou, O Lord our God, king of the universe, who
chose us from every people, and exalted us among every tongue,
and sanctified us by his commandments. With love hast thou given
us, O Lord our God, holidays for gladness, [Sabbaths for rest]
festivals and seasons for rejoicing, this [Sabbath day and this] day

---

THE KIDDUSH

The cup of wine over which the Kiddush is chanted, is the first of the four
cups prescribed for the Seder. The Kiddush follows the general usage on other
festivals.

An ancient regulation requires that the hands be washed whenever food is
dipped into a liquid (Pesahim 115a). Although it has fallen into general disuse,
the authorities have insisted on including this practice in the Seder ritual. In some
countries only the master of the Seder is required to wash his hands, in others only
the male participants.

The afikoman is usually concealed under a pillow, evidently to prevent its
being accidentally eaten during the meal.

The custom of dividing the matzah at this point in the Seder is already found
in Mahzor Vitry. The Siddur Rav Amram is unacquainted with this custom; so
is Maimonides who calls for dividing the matzah immediately before the meal.
Evidently our custom is a relic of the ancient practice of beginning the meal at this
point.

וְאֶת־יוֹם] חַג הַמַּצּוֹת הַזֶּה זְמַן חֵרוּתֵנוּ [בְּאַהֲבָה] מִקְרָא־קֹדֶשׁ זֵכֶר לִיצִיאַת מִצְרָיִם. כִּי בָנוּ בָחַרְתָּ וְאוֹתָנוּ קִדַּשְׁתָּ מִכָּל־הָעַמִּים [וְשַׁבָּת] וּמוֹעֲדֵי קָדְשֶׁךָ [בְּאַהֲבָה וּבְרָצוֹן] בְּשִׂמְחָה וּבְשָׂשׂוֹן הִנְחַלְתָּנוּ. בָּרוּךְ אַתָּה יְיָ מְקַדֵּשׁ [הַשַּׁבָּת וְ]יִשְׂרָאֵל וְהַזְּמַנִּים:

The following is recited at the close of the Sabbath:

[וּ]בָּרוּךְ אַתָּה יְיָ אֱלֹהֵינוּ מֶלֶךְ הָעוֹלָם. בּוֹרֵא מְאוֹרֵי הָאֵשׁ:

בָּרוּךְ אַתָּה יְיָ אֱלֹהֵינוּ מֶלֶךְ הָעוֹלָם. הַמַּבְדִּיל בֵּין קֹדֶשׁ לְחוֹל. בֵּין אוֹר לְחשֶׁךְ. בֵּין יִשְׂרָאֵל לָעַמִּים. בֵּין יוֹם הַשְּׁבִיעִי לְשֵׁשֶׁת יְמֵי הַמַּעֲשֶׂה: בֵּין קְדֻשַּׁת שַׁבָּת לִקְדֻשַּׁת יוֹם טוֹב הִבְדַּלְתָּ וְאֶת־יוֹם הַשְּׁבִיעִי מִשֵּׁשֶׁת יְמֵי־הַמַּעֲשֶׂה קִדַּשְׁתָּ. הִבְדַּלְתָּ וְקִדַּשְׁתָּ אֶת־עַמְּךָ יִשְׂרָאֵל בִּקְדֻשָּׁתֶךָ. בָּרוּךְ אַתָּה יְיָ הַמַּבְדִּיל בֵּין קֹדֶשׁ לְקֹדֶשׁ:

בָּרוּךְ אַתָּה יְיָ אֱלֹהֵינוּ מֶלֶךְ הָעוֹלָם. שֶׁהֶחֱיָנוּ. וְקִיְּמָנוּ. וְהִגִּיעָנוּ לַזְּמַן הַזֶּה:

The first cup of wine is drunk in a reclining position.

וּרְחַץ

Pitcher, basin, and towel are offered to the master of the Seder to wash his hands, though without saying the usual benediction over the washing of hands.

כַּרְפַּס

The master of the Seder dips some celery or other vegetable in salt water (or vinegar) and then offers a piece of the vegetable to each participant. The following benediction is spoken before eating the *karpas*.

בָּרוּךְ אַתָּה יְיָ אֱלֹהֵינוּ מֶלֶךְ הָעוֹלָם. בּוֹרֵא פְּרִי הָאֲדָמָה:

יַחַץ

The master of the Seder breaks in two the middle of the three wafers of unleavened bread on the platter, wraps up the larger half in a cloth and sets it aside for the *afikoman*.

of the festival of unleavened bread, the season of our deliverance, [with love] a holy convocation in remembrance of the departure from Egypt. For us hast thou chosen, and us hast thou sanctified from all the peoples. [And the Sabbath] And the holidays of thy sanctification [with love and favor] hast thou given us, with gladness and joy to inherit. Blessed art thou, O Lord, who sanctifies [the Sabbath and] Israel and the seasons.

The following is recited at the close of the Sabbath:

[Blessed art thou, O Lord our God, king of the universe, creator of the light of the fire.

Blessed art thou, O Lord our God, king of the universe, who divides the holy from the profane, light from darkness, Israel from the nations, the seventh day from the six days of work; the sanctity of the Sabbath from the sanctity of the holiday hast thou divided, and hast sanctified the seventh day above the six days of work. Thou hast set apart and hallowed thy people Israel with thy sanctity. Blessed art thou, O Lord, who divides sanctity from sanctity.]

Blessed art thou, O Lord our God, king of the universe, who has kept us alive, and sustained us, and enabled us to reach this season.

The first cup of wine is drunk in a reclining position.

Pitcher, basin, and towel are offered to the participants in the Seder to wash their hands, though without saying the usual benediction over the washing of hands.

The master of the Seder dips some celery or other vegetable in salt water (or vinegar) and then offers a piece of the vegetable to each participant. The following benediction is spoken before eating the *karpas*.

Blessed art thou, O Lord our God, king of the universe, who creates the fruit of the earth.

The master of the Seder breaks in two the middle of the three wafers of unleavened bread on the platter, wraps up the larger half in a cloth and sets it aside for the *afikoman*.

Baking the matzoh. The women are dressed in saris. Captions are in Marathi, the mother tongue of the Bene Israel of Bombay. Poona, India, 1874 (JTSAL).

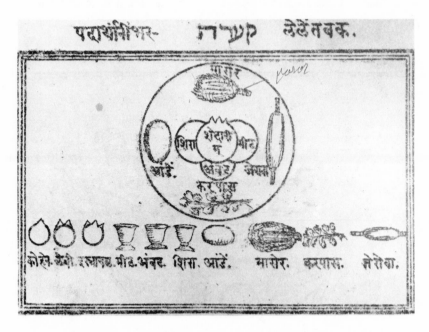

The seder plate, Marathi translation. Poona, India, 1874 (JTSAL).

Title page featuring Moses before the burning bush, above, and
Moses and Aaron, below. Bombay, India, 1846 (JTSAL).

The master of the Seder removes the shankbone (*zeroa*) and the egg from the platter; those sitting near him lift up the platter and all the company recite:

הָא לַחְמָא עַנְיָא דִי־אֲכָלוּ אַבְהָתָנָא בְּאַרְעָא דְמִצְרָיִם. כָּל־דִכְפִין יֵיתֵי וְיֵכוֹל. כָּל־דִצְרִיךְ יֵיתֵי וְיִפְסַח. הָשַׁתָּא הָכָא. לְשָׁנָה הַבָּאָה בְּאַרְעָא דְיִשְׂרָאֵל. הָשַׁתָּא עַבְדֵי. לְשָׁנָה הַבָּאָה בְּנֵי חוֹרִין:

The platter is put back on the table, and the second cup of wine poured. The youngest child or another participant asks the Four Questions.

מַה־נִּשְׁתַּנָּה הַלַּיְלָה הַזֶּה מִכָּל־הַלֵּילוֹת. שֶׁבְּכָל־הַלֵּילוֹת אָנוּ אוֹכְלִין חָמֵץ וּמַצָּה. הַלַּיְלָה הַזֶּה כֻּלּוֹ מַצָּה:

שֶׁבְּכָל־הַלֵּילוֹת אָנוּ אוֹכְלִין שְׁאָר יְרָקוֹת. הַלַּיְלָה הַזֶּה מָרוֹר:

שֶׁבְּכָל־הַלֵּילוֹת אֵין אָנוּ מַטְבִּילִין אֲפִילוּ פַּעַם אָחָת. הַלַּיְלָה הַזֶּה שְׁתֵּי פְעָמִים:

שֶׁבְּכָל־הַלֵּילוֹת אָנוּ אוֹכְלִין בֵּין יוֹשְׁבִין וּבֵין מְסֻבִּין. הַלַּיְלָה הַזֶּה כֻּלָּנוּ מְסֻבִּין:

THE INTRODUCTION

This is one of the oldest parts of the Haggadah.

The Aramaic language, in which this passage is written, was the language spoken in Palestine mainly in the time of the Second Temple. The reference to the "Passover feast," or rather, to the Passover sacrifice, suggests that the passage was written before the destruction of the Temple. The few Hebrew words which occur in the Aramaic text possibly derive, as in the Kaddish and the Kol Nidre, from a parallel Hebrew version. A pure Aramaic version is preserved in the Mahzor Roma and Mahzor Romania. Since it contains an invitation to the poor to participate in the Seder, it might more properly have been placed before the Kiddush. However, it is meant to be a prologue to the Haggadah proper, of which the Kiddush, recited on all the other festivals as well, is not an integral part.

the bread of poverty which our forefathers ate in the land of Egypt: i. e., while

The master of the Seder removes the shankbone (*zeroa*) and
the egg from the platter; those sitting near him lift up the
platter and all the company recite:

THE INTRODUCTION

This is the bread of poverty which our forefathers ate in the land of
Egypt. Let all who are hungry enter and eat; let all who are needy
come to our Passover feast. This year we are here; next year may
we be in the Land of Israel. This year we are slaves; next year may
we be free men.

The platter is put back on the table, and the second cup of wine
poured. The youngest child or another participant asks the
Four Questions.

THE FOUR QUESTIONS

Why does this night differ from all other nights? For on all other
nights we eat either leavened or unleavened bread; why on this
night only unleavened bread?

On all other nights we eat all kinds of herbs; why on this night only
bitter herbs?

On all other nights we need not dip our herbs even once; why on
this night must we dip them twice?

On all other nights we eat either sitting up or reclining; why on
this night do we all recline?

---

going out of Egypt. Some medieval commentators assumed that the Jews ate
unleavened bread during their slavery in Egypt.

next year may we be in the Land of Israel: This phrase at the beginning of the
Haggadah corresponds to its closing prayer: *Next year in Jerusalem!* The hope for
a return to Zion was emphasized on Passover in accordance with the midrashic
tradition: "Nisan is the month of redemption; in Nisan Israel was redeemed from
Egypt; in Nisan Israel will again be redeemed" (Exodus Rabbah XV. 12).

THE FOUR QUESTIONS

For a better understanding of the questions the original order of the Seder
should be kept in mind: the hors d'oeuvre, wine, and the main meal; and only then
the reading of the Haggadah. The child was to express surprise over at least three

עֲבָדִים הָיִינוּ לְפַרְעֹה בְּמִצְרָיִם. וַיּוֹצִיאֵנוּ יְיָ אֱלֹהֵינוּ מִשָּׁם בְּיָד
חֲזָקָה וּבִזְרוֹעַ נְטוּיָה: וְאִלּוּ לֹא הוֹצִיא הַקָּדוֹשׁ בָּרוּךְ הוּא אֶת־אֲבוֹתֵינוּ
מִמִּצְרָיִם. הֲרֵי אָנוּ וּבָנֵינוּ וּבְנֵי בָנֵינוּ מְשֻׁעְבָּדִים הָיִינוּ לְפַרְעֹה בְּמִצְרָיִם.
וַאֲפִילוּ כֻּלָּנוּ חֲכָמִים. כֻּלָּנוּ נְבוֹנִים. כֻּלָּנוּ זְקֵנִים. כֻּלָּנוּ יוֹדְעִים אֶת־
הַתּוֹרָה. מִצְוָה עָלֵינוּ לְסַפֵּר בִּיצִיאַת מִצְרָיִם. וְכָל־הַמַּרְבֶּה לְסַפֵּר
בִּיצִיאַת מִצְרַיִם הֲרֵי זֶה מְשֻׁבָּח:

מַעֲשֶׂה בְּרַבִּי אֱלִיעֶזֶר וְרַבִּי יְהוֹשֻׁעַ וְרַבִּי אֶלְעָזָר בֶּן־עֲזַרְיָה וְרַבִּי
עֲקִיבָא וְרַבִּי טַרְפוֹן שֶׁהָיוּ מְסֻבִּין בִּבְנֵי בְרַק. וְהָיוּ מְסַפְּרִים בִּיצִיאַת

---

departures from the usual course of the meal: first that dipped vegetables were
eaten twice (as hors d'oeuvre, when *karpas* is dipped in salt water, and during the
main meal when the bitter herbs are dipped in *haroset*), not, as ordinarily, only
once; second, that only unleavened bread was eaten; and third, referring to the
period of the Temple, that the meat of the paschal lamb was roasted and not
stewed or boiled. This is the form in which the — originally three — questions
were formulated in the Palestinian Mishnah, and they correspond logically to the
early order of the Seder. After the cessation of the sacrifices the third question
was, or course, omitted.

After the ancient custom of eating dipped vegetables as hors d'oeuvres before
the regular meal fell into disuse, it was still retained for the Seder meal in order to
capture the attention of the children. Consequently, the question had to be re-
phrased to read: *On all other nights we need not dip our herbs even once; why on this
night must we dip them twice?* Since the bitter herbs were not here expressly mentioned, another phrase was added: *On all other nights we eat all kinds of herbs; why
on this night only bitter herbs?*

The last question, about the reason for reclining, would have been meaningless
in ancient times and stems from the post-talmudic period. The questions as formulated in the Mishnah were intended to serve as models; they could be replaced by
others (Pesahim 115b; 116b).

Current usage requires that they be asked by the youngest participant at the
Seder. When only husband and wife are present, the wife asks the questions; in
case an individual is compelled to perform the Seder alone, he must read the questions to himself. "Even two scholars who know the laws of Passover ask one

The master of the Seder and all the celebrants recite the Reply.

We were Pharaoh's slaves in Egypt, and the Lord our God brought us forth from there with a mighty hand and an outstretched arm. And if the Holy One, blessed be he, had not brought our forefathers forth from Egypt, then we, our children, and our children's children would still be Pharaoh's slaves in Egypt.

So, even though all of us were wise, all of us full of understanding, all of us elders, all of us knowing in the Torah, we should still be under the commandment to tell the story of the departure from Egypt. And the more one tells the story of the departure from Egypt, the more praiseworthy he is.

A tale is told of Rabbi Eliezer, Rabbi Joshua, Rabbi Eleazar ben Azariah, Rabbi Akiba, and Rabbi Tarfon, who once reclined together at Bene Berak telling about the departure from Egypt all night, until

---

another the questions" (Pesahim 116a). Not all authorities consider the youngest participant the reader of the questions. Maimonides (12th cent.) requires that the questions be recited by the master of the Seder, while the school of Rashi (11th cent.) suggests that the master at least explain them in the vernacular.[1]

THE REPLY

The Mishnah (Pesahim X.4) requires that the core of the Reply, a midrashic commentary on Deut. 26:5-8, is to be preceded by an introductory statement which "begins with the humiliation and ends with the glory." There are two differing traditions as to such an introductory statement (Pesahim 116a). Our Haggadah records first the talmudic tradition upheld by Samuel, who introduces the Reply with the verse, *We were Pharaoh's slaves.* According to the other tradition (upheld by Rav), the Reply should begin with the verse, *In the beginning our fathers were idolators*; this text is later quoted in our Haggadah.

wise . . . full of understanding . . . knowing in the Torah: Three expressions current in the Wisdom literature. *All of us elders*, absent from many rituals, is of later origin.

A tale is told: This tale is repeated nowhere else in the rabbinic literature. The rabbis mentioned here lived from *ca.* 100 to *ca.* 130 C. E., one generation after the

[1] Maimonides, Mishneh Torah, Hametz u-Matzah VIII.2. For the school of Rashi, see Sefer ha-Pardes 133; Mahzor Vitry, p. 295.

מִצְרַיִם כָּל־אוֹתוֹ הַלַּיְלָה. עַד־שֶׁבָּאוּ תַלְמִידֵיהֶם וְאָמְרוּ לָהֶם. רַבּוֹתֵינוּ. הִגִּיעַ זְמַן קְרִיאַת שְׁמַע שֶׁל־שַׁחֲרִית:

אָמַר רַבִּי אֶלְעָזָר בָּן־עֲזַרְיָה. הֲרֵי אֲנִי כְּבֶן־שִׁבְעִים שָׁנָה. וְלֹא זָכִיתִי שֶׁתֵּאָמֵר יְצִיאַת מִצְרַיִם בַּלֵּילוֹת. עַד שֶׁדְּרָשָׁהּ בֶּן־זוֹמָא. שֶׁנֶּאֱמַר: לְמַעַן תִּזְכֹּר אֶת־יוֹם צֵאתְךָ מֵאֶרֶץ מִצְרַיִם כֹּל יְמֵי חַיֶּיךָ: יְמֵי חַיֶּיךָ הַיָּמִים. כֹּל יְמֵי חַיֶּיךָ הַלֵּילוֹת. וַחֲכָמִים אוֹמְרִים יְמֵי חַיֶּיךָ הָעוֹלָם הַזֶּה. כֹּל יְמֵי חַיֶּיךָ לְהָבִיא לִימוֹת הַמָּשִׁיחַ:

בָּרוּךְ הַמָּקוֹם בָּרוּךְ הוּא [בָּרוּךְ] שֶׁנָּתַן תּוֹרָה לְעַמּוֹ יִשְׂרָאֵל [בָּרוּךְ הוּא]:

כְּנֶגֶד אַרְבָּעָה בָנִים דִּבְּרָה תוֹרָה. אֶחָד חָכָם. וְאֶחָד רָשָׁע. וְאֶחָד תָּם. וְאֶחָד שֶׁאֵינוֹ יוֹדֵעַ לִשְׁאוֹל:

---

fall of the Second Temple. Bene Berak, the residence of Rabbi Akiba is a village in Judea, south-east of Jaffa. The liberation from Egypt may have been intended as a cryptic reference to the liberation from Rome, *the* political issue at the time of Rabbi Akiba. It was Rabbi Akiba who took part in the Bar Kokhba rebellion against Rome in 132. A similar story is told (Tosefta Pesahim X. 12) of Rabban Gamaliel and the elders at Lydda, an important Jewish center in 2nd cent. Palestine (today the airport of Israel).

Rabbi Eleazar ben Azariah said: Rabbi Eleazar's dictum is presented as if it dealt with a subject of the above-mentioned session at Bene Berak, and as if it referred solely to the Passover evening. In its original context, however (Mishnah Berakhot I.5; Sifre Deuteronomy 130; Mekhilta on 13:3), this passage discussed the question whether the exodus from Egypt (as contained in the third section of the *shema*) should be mentioned in the daytime prayer, or in the evening prayer as well.

THE FOUR SONS

This passage, a midrashic exposition of Deut. 6:20–24 (or Exod. 13:14), is an illustration to the Mishnah's dictum: "According to the understanding of the son doth his father instruct him" (Pesahim X. 4).

their disciples came to them and said, "Masters, the time has come to read the morning *shema*."

Rabbi Eleazar ben Azariah said: "Lo, I am like a man of seventy years, yet I never understood why the story concerning the departure from Egypt should be recited at night, until Ben Zoma interpreted it so. So it is said [Deut. 16:3]: 'That thou mayest remember the day when thou camest forth out of the land of Egypt all the days of thy life." Had it been written 'the days of thy life,' it would have meant the days only; but 'all the days of thy life' means the nights as well."

The other sages explain the verse differently: "Had it been written 'the days of thy life,' it would have meant this world only; 'all the days of thy life' means that the times of the Messiah are included as well."

THE FOUR SONS

Blessed be the Omnipresent, blessed be he, who gave the Torah to his people Israel.

The Torah has four children in mind: one, intelligent, a second, wicked, a third, simple, and a fourth, a child that does not yet know how to ask.

Both the composition and contents of this section present considerable textual difficulties.[2] We shall restrict our remarks to a simple explanation of our text.

Blessed be the Omnipresent: An introductory formula current in the midrashim of the post-talmudic times.

the Omnipresent blessed be he is a *single* phrase, comparable to the Holy One, blessed be he. The designation of the Deity as *makom*, lit., "Place" (with or without the addition "blessed be he"), already found in the Mishnah, has been explained as meaning: "He is the Place of the world and the world is not His place" (Genesis Rabbah LXVIII. 9).

As to the contents of the midrash: There are four scriptural passages which bid the father to instruct his son in reference to Passover.

[2] See Introduction to the Hebrew Haggadah commentary by Daniel [E. D.] Goldschmidt, Jerusalem 1947. For a comprehensive discussion of this passage, see L. Finkelstein, *Harvard Theological Review* (hereinafter HTR) XXXVI (1943), 8 ff.

צורת ארבעה בנים דברה תורה

TOP: The four sons. Sulzbach, Bavaria, 1711 (JTSAL).
BOTTOM: The four sons. Woodcut based on the earlier copperplate
etching shown above. Offenbach, Germany, 1722 (JTSAL).

The four sons. Prague, 1526 (JTSAL).

חָכָם מַה הוּא אוֹמֵר. מָה הָעֵדֹת וְהַחֻקִּים וְהַמִּשְׁפָּטִים אֲשֶׁר צִוָּה יְיָ אֱלֹהֵינוּ אֶתְכֶם: וְאַף אַתָּה אֱמוֹר לוֹ כְּהִלְכוֹת הַפֶּסַח. אֵין מַפְטִירִין אַחַר הַפֶּסַח אֲפִיקוֹמָן:

רָשָׁע מַה הוּא אוֹמֵר. מָה הָעֲבוֹדָה הַזֹּאת לָכֶם: לָכֶם וְלֹא לוֹ. וּלְפִי שֶׁהוֹצִיא אֶת־עַצְמוֹ מִן־הַכְּלָל וְכָפַר בָּעִקָּר. אַף אַתָּה הַקְהֵה אֶת־שִׁנָּיו וֶאֱמוֹר לוֹ. בַּעֲבוּר זֶה עָשָׂה יְיָ לִי בְּצֵאתִי מִמִּצְרָיִם: לִי וְלֹא לוֹ. אִלּוּ הָיָה שָׁם לֹא הָיָה נִגְאָל:

תָּם מַה הוּא אוֹמֵר. מַה־זֹּאת. וְאָמַרְתָּ אֵלָיו. בְּחֹזֶק יָד הוֹצִיאָנוּ יְיָ מִמִּצְרַיִם מִבֵּית עֲבָדִים:

---

1. Deut. 6:20-24: The son who inquires intelligently about the meaning of the laws is to be given a detailed answer, going back to the exodus from Egypt, and the conquest of the land of Israel. 2. Exod. 12:26 ff.: When children express their curiosity about the customs of the paschal sacrifice with the question, '*What mean ye by this service?*' they are to be given a brief historical explanation. As quoted in the Torah, this question is by no means framed in a spirit of contempt. 3. Exod. 13:14: The son who inquires about the meaning of the "redemption" of the first-born is to be instructed in the part the first-born had played in the deliverance from Egypt and in the particulars of the law of "redemption." 4. Exod. 13:8: The father is obliged to teach the Passover precepts to his son even without a previous question on the child's part. The midrash, which refers all four verses to the precepts of the Passover, takes the formulation of the questions as an indication of the intelligence and religious attitude of the inquiring child.

What does the intelligent child say? The thoroughness of his question testifies to the child's keen interest. Of the categories here mentioned, "statutes," according to talmudic tradition, are laws the reason for which are not apparent; and "ordinances" those which are self-evident; the meaning of "testimonies" in this context is not definite.

hath commanded you: The ancient sources of this midrash as well as old versions of the Haggadah quote the verse as reading: ". . . which our God hath commanded us," which is also the reading of the Septuagint translation. This version makes the contrast between the question of the intelligent son and that of the wicked apparent. In the Middle Ages the masoretic reading "hath commanded you" was

What does the intelligent child say, "What mean the testimonies, and the statutes, and the ordinances which the Lord our God hath commanded you?" [Deut. 6:20].

And you instruct him in the precepts of Passover, to wit: "One may not conclude after the Paschal meal (by saying), 'Now to the entertainment!'"

What does the wicked child say, "What is this service to you?" "To you," and not to him. Since he removes himself from the group, and so denies God, you in return must set his teeth on edge, and answer him: "It is because of that which the Lord did for me when I came forth from Egypt" [Exod. 13:8]. "For me," not for him. Had he been there, he would not have been redeemed.

What does the simple child say? "What is this?" And thou shalt say to him: "By strength of hand the Lord brought us out from Egypt, from the house of bondage" [Exod. 13:14].

---

introduced into the Haggadah text. Commentators, then, tried to explain why the phrase "you," used by both the wise and the wicked in their questions, militates against the wicked son but not against the intelligent. This difficulty does not arise if we maintain the old Haggadah reading: "hath commanded us."

One may not conclude: This is a passage toward the end of Mishnah Pesahim X, a chapter which — as indicated above — deals with the Seder in the mishnaic times. The meaning of the answer to the intelligent son is: Teach him all the Passover precepts through the last passage in the Mishnah text which might interest him: the one beginning, "One may not conclude."

entertainment (*afikoman*): Correctly, *epikomios*, a Greek word meaning festival procession; the meaning is already uncertain in the Talmud, where it is variously explained as "dessert," "dinner music," and "the practice of going from one company to another" (Pesahim 119b; Yerushalmi Pesahim 37d). The term covers the after-dinner revelry which was a customary sequel to the ancient banquet, especially for the young. The sages prohibited the *afikoman* on the Passover night so that attention be not diverted from the paschal sacrifice.

What does the wicked child say? The baseness of the wicked child is expressed in the phrase "to you" (in its literal sense quite harmless), with which the inquirer dissociates himself as it were from the community. The Palestinian Talmud has this version: "What is all this trouble you make us every year!"

וְשֶׁאֵינוֹ יוֹדֵעַ לִשְׁאוֹל אַתְּ פְּתַח לוֹ. שֶׁנֶּאֱמַר: וְהִגַּדְתָּ לְבִנְךָ בַּיּוֹם
הַהוּא לֵאמֹר. בַּעֲבוּר זֶה עָשָׂה יְיָ לִי בְּצֵאתִי מִמִּצְרָיִם:

יָכוֹל מֵרֹאשׁ חֹדֶשׁ. תַּלְמוּד לוֹמַר בַּיּוֹם הַהוּא. אִי בַּיּוֹם הַהוּא
יָכוֹל מִבְּעוֹד יוֹם. תַּלְמוּד לוֹמַר בַּעֲבוּר זֶה. בַּעֲבוּר זֶה לֹא אָמַרְתִּי
אֶלָּא בְּשָׁעָה שֶׁיֵּשׁ מַצָּה וּמָרוֹר מֻנָּחִים לְפָנֶיךָ:

מִתְּחִלָּה עוֹבְדֵי עֲבוֹדָה זָרָה הָיוּ אֲבוֹתֵינוּ. וְעַכְשָׁו קֵרְבָנוּ הַמָּקוֹם
לַעֲבוֹדָתוֹ. שֶׁנֶּאֱמַר: וַיֹּאמֶר יְהוֹשֻׁעַ אֶל־כָּל־הָעָם. כֹּה אָמַר יְיָ אֱלֹהֵי
יִשְׂרָאֵל בְּעֵבֶר הַנָּהָר יָשְׁבוּ אֲבוֹתֵיכֶם מֵעוֹלָם תֶּרַח אֲבִי אַבְרָהָם
וַאֲבִי נָחוֹר וַיַּעַבְדוּ אֱלֹהִים אֲחֵרִים: וָאֶקַּח אֶת־אֲבִיכֶם אֶת־אַבְרָהָם
מֵעֵבֶר הַנָּהָר. וָאוֹלֵךְ אוֹתוֹ בְּכָל־אֶרֶץ כְּנָעַן וָאַרְבֶּה אֶת־זַרְעוֹ וָאֶתֶּן־לוֹ
אֶת־יִצְחָק: וָאֶתֵּן לְיִצְחָק אֶת־יַעֲקֹב וְאֶת־עֵשָׂו. וָאֶתֵּן לְעֵשָׂו אֶת־הַר שֵׂעִיר
לָרֶשֶׁת אוֹתוֹ וְיַעֲקֹב וּבָנָיו יָרְדוּ מִצְרָיִם:

"And I took your father Abraham from beyond
the River"

And with him who does not know how to ask: The absence of a question in
the scriptural verse is an indication that the child is not yet mature enough to
inquire.

And with him who does not know how to ask you must open and begin yourself. "And thou shalt tell thy son in that day, saying: It is because of that which the Lord did for me when I came forth out of Egypt" [Exod. 13:8].

"And thou shalt tell thy son . . .": It might have been thought that the telling should begin on the first day of the month [of Nisan]: therefore the text teaches us "in that day." But since it says "in that day," we might have thought that we should begin while it is still day; therefore the Scripture also teaches us "because of that." You could not say "because of *that*," if it were not referring to the time when unleavened bread and bitter herbs were lying before you.

In the beginning our fathers were idolators, but now the Omnipresent has drawn us to his service, as it is said: "And Joshua said unto all the people: 'Thus saith the Lord, the God of Israel: Your fathers dwelt of old time beyond the River, even Terah, the father of Abraham, and the father of Nahor; and they served other gods. And I took your father Abraham from beyond the River, and led him throughout all the land of Canaan, and multiplied his seed, and gave him Isaac. And I gave unto Isaac Jacob and Esau; and I gave unto Esau Mount Seir, to possess it; and Jacob and his children went down into Egypt' " [Josh. 24:2–4].

You must open: The feminine form of you (*at*) is possibly an Aramaism. Heidenheim and others substitute the masculine form (*atta*).

It might have been thought: This homily, found in the Mekhilta on Exod. 13:8 refers to all the sons. Since it is customary to begin preparing for the festival some weeks in advance, the question is raised whether the father should not also begin instructing his children before the holiday.

because of that: Here the father points to paschal lamb, unleavened bread, and bitter herbs lying before him.

In the beginning: This is Rav's version of the introductory statement to the Reply, as against Samuel's version, quoted before ("We were Pharaoh's slaves").

ויאמר יהושע אל כל העם כה אמר ה' אלהי ישראל בעב. הנהר ישבו אבותיכם מעולם תרח אבי אברהם ואבי
נחור ויעבדו אלהים אחרים :

וישא עיניו וירא והגה שלשה אנשים נצבים עליו   ויעבר אברם בארץ

TOP: Abraham smashing his father's idols. Offenbach, Germany, 1722 (JTSAL).
BOTTOM: The three angels visit Abraham and Sarah.
Offenbach, Germany, 1722 (JTSAL).

וישלכהו ארצה ויהי לנחש   ויאמרו אל פרעה כה אמר ה'

י א

ויגער ה' את מצרים בתוך הים   ובני ישראל הלכו ביבשה בתוך הים

TOP: Moses, Aaron, and the magicians turning rods into snakes
before Pharaoh. Offenbach, Germany, 1722 (JTSAL).
BOTTOM: The drowning of the Egyptians in the Red Sea.
Offenbach, Germany, 1722 (JTSAL).

37

בָּרוּךְ שׁוֹמֵר הַבְטָחָתוֹ לְיִשְׂרָאֵל. בָּרוּךְ הוּא. שֶׁהַקָּדוֹשׁ בָּרוּךְ הוּא
חִשֵּׁב אֶת־הַקֵּץ לַעֲשׂוֹת כְּמָה שֶׁאָמַר לְאַבְרָהָם אָבִינוּ בִּבְרִית בֵּין
הַבְּתָרִים. שֶׁנֶּאֱמַר: וַיֹּאמֶר לְאַבְרָם יָדֹעַ תֵּדַע כִּי־גֵר יִהְיֶה זַרְעֲךָ בְּאֶרֶץ
לֹא לָהֶם וַעֲבָדוּם וְעִנּוּ אֹתָם אַרְבַּע מֵאוֹת שָׁנָה: וְגַם אֶת־הַגּוֹי אֲשֶׁר
יַעֲבֹדוּ דָּן אָנֹכִי. וְאַחֲרֵי־כֵן יֵצְאוּ בִּרְכֻשׁ גָּדוֹל:

The participants lift up their cups of wine and say:

וְהִיא שֶׁעָמְדָה לַאֲבוֹתֵינוּ וְלָנוּ. שֶׁלֹּא אֶחָד בִּלְבַד עָמַד עָלֵינוּ [לְכַלּוֹתֵנוּ].
אֶלָּא שֶׁבְּכָל־דּוֹר וָדוֹר עוֹמְדִים עָלֵינוּ לְכַלּוֹתֵנוּ. וְהַקָּדוֹשׁ בָּרוּךְ הוּא
מַצִּילֵנוּ מִיָּדָם:

The cups are put back on the table.

צֵא וּלְמַד מַה־בִּקֵּשׁ לָבָן הָאֲרַמִּי לַעֲשׂוֹת לְיַעֲקֹב אָבִינוּ. שֶׁפַּרְעֹה
לֹא גָזַר אֶלָּא עַל־הַזְּכָרִים. וְלָבָן בִּקֵּשׁ לַעֲקוֹר אֶת־הַכֹּל. שֶׁנֶּאֱמַר:

THE MIDRASH ON DEUT. 26:5–8

According to the Mishnah Pesahim, this midrash constitutes the core of the
Haggadah. It is a running commentary on a few verses in Deut. (26:5–8) which
were very familiar to the ancient Jews as part of a confessional annually recited
by pilgrims bringing their first fruits to the Temple at Shavuot, the Feast of Weeks.
The midrash proper is preceded by a benedictory phrase.

the Covenant between the Sections: A name derived from the description of the
sacrificial rite which accompanied the making of the covenant of Abraham (Gen.
15:9).

four hundred years: Or, 430, according to Exod. 12:40. The commentators
let this period begin with the birth of Isaac or the Covenant itself, so that the actual
stay in Egypt lasted only 210 years.[3]

[3] Cf. Ibn Ezra and Biur on Gen. 15:13; Yalkut Shimeoni, Genesis 77, according to
which *hishev et ha-ketz* means "he deducted 190 (the numerical value of *ketz*) years
(from the 400)."

INTRODUCTION

Blessed be He who keeps his promise to Israel, blessed be he. For the Holy One, blessed be he, premeditated the end of the bondage, thus doing that which he said to Abraham in the Covenant between the Sections, as it is said: "And he said unto Abram: 'Know of a surety that thy seed shall be a stranger in a land that is not theirs, and shall serve them; and they shall afflict them four hundred years; and also that nation, whom they shall serve, will I judge; and afterward shall they come out with great substance'" [Gen. 15:13-14].

The participants lift up their cups of wine and say:

And it is this promise which has stood by our fathers and by us. For it was not one man only who stood up against us to destroy us; in every generation they stand up against us to destroy us, and the Holy One, blessed be he, saves us from their hand.

The cups are put back on the table.

Go forth and learn what Laban, the Aramean, sought to do to Jacob, our father. While Pharaoh decreed death only for the male children, Laban sought to uproot all.

Pharaoh: See Exod. 1:16, 22; Sotah 12a; Exodus Rabbah I. 13. Laban: *see* Gen. 31:29. It is strange that the exposition of the exodus story should begin with a declaration that Laban was even worse than Pharaoh. Louis Finkelstein tries to prove that this midrash was pre-Maccabean, and was composed in the 3rd cent. B. C. E. when Palestine was ruled by the Ptolemies. He points out that it reflects the struggle between Syria and Egypt to dominate Palestine. Laban, in typical midrashic style, represents the Syrian king. Since Passover is thoroughly anti-Egyptian in spirit, some gesture was necessary to placate the Egyptian rulers; hence the denunciation of Laban as a greater enemy of Israel than Pharaoh.[4]

[4] In HTR XXXI, pp. 291-317. Daniel [E. D.] Goldschmidt (Hebrew Haggadah commentary, p. 16, n. 1) does not find it possible fully to agree with this interpretation.

אֲרַמִּי אֹבֵד אָבִי וַיֵּרֶד מִצְרַיְמָה וַיָּגָר שָׁם בִּמְתֵי מְעָט. וַיְהִי־שָׁם לְגוֹי גָּדוֹל עָצוּם וָרָב:

וַיֵּרֶד מִצְרַיְמָה. אָנוּס עַל־פִּי הַדִּבּוּר: וַיָּגָר שָׁם. מְלַמֵּד שֶׁלֹּא יָרַד לְהִשְׁתַּקֵּעַ בְּמִצְרַיִם אֶלָּא לָגוּר שָׁם. שֶׁנֶּאֱמַר: וַיֹּאמְרוּ אֶל־פַּרְעֹה לָגוּר בָּאָרֶץ בָּאנוּ כִּי־אֵין מִרְעֶה לַצֹּאן אֲשֶׁר לַעֲבָדֶיךָ כִּי־כָבֵד הָרָעָב בְּאֶרֶץ כְּנָעַן. וְעַתָּה יֵשְׁבוּ־נָא עֲבָדֶיךָ בְּאֶרֶץ גֹּשֶׁן:

בִּמְתֵי מְעָט. כְּמָה שֶׁנֶּאֱמַר: בְּשִׁבְעִים נֶפֶשׁ יָרְדוּ אֲבֹתֶיךָ מִצְרַיְמָה. וְעַתָּה שָׂמְךָ יְיָ אֱלֹהֶיךָ כְּכוֹכְבֵי הַשָּׁמַיִם לָרֹב: וַיְהִי־שָׁם לְגוֹי. מְלַמֵּד שֶׁהָיוּ יִשְׂרָאֵל מְצֻיָּנִים שָׁם: גָּדוֹל עָצוּם. כְּמָה שֶׁנֶּאֱמַר. וּבְנֵי יִשְׂרָאֵל פָּרוּ וַיִּשְׁרְצוּ וַיִּרְבּוּ וַיַּעַצְמוּ בִּמְאֹד מְאֹד. וַתִּמָּלֵא הָאָרֶץ אֹתָם:

An Aramean would have destroyed my father: Our translation implies the midrashic interpretation which has "Aramean" refer to Laban, "my father" to Jacob Literally, the verse should be rendered as, "A wandering Aramean was my father." Jacob was called an Aramean because he spent many years in Aram, besides being the son of Rebecca, who was born there. The midrash is unwilling, however, to identify Jacob as an Aramean, a designation usually reserved in the Pentateuch for Laban. It consequently reads or interprets the word *oved* "wandering" as *ibbed*, "would have destroyed."

After prefacing the cited verse with a remark about Laban's wickedness, the homilist then proceeds to quote the passage a verse at a time, commenting on each successive phrase. The homily now deals directly with the subject of the celebration, the redemption from Egyptian bondage. Although the Mishnah (Pesahim X. 4) specifically prescribes that the entire confessional mentioned above be expounded, the Haggadah omits the last two verses which begin, "And he hath brought us into this place, and hath given us this land, a land flowing with milk and honey." Evidently, after the destruction of the Second Temple and the dispersion these verses could no longer be included in the confessional. Most of the midrashic analysis quotes corresponding passages from other parts of the Scripture (introduced by the words "As it is said") as proof of or as illustration to the phrase to be interpreted.

compelled: We have no biblical proof for this statement. Some commentators think of the permission granted Jacob to go down to Egypt (Gen. 46:3-4) as

For it is said: "An Aramean would have destroyed my father, and he went down into Egypt, and sojourned there, few in number; and he became there a nation, great, mighty, and populous" [cf. Deut. 26:5].

"And he went down into Egypt": compelled by the word of God. "And sojourned there": teaching us that Jacob did not go down to Egypt to settle but to sojourn there. As it is said: "And they said unto Pharaoh: 'To sojourn in the land are we come; for there is no pasture for thy servants' flocks; for the famine is sore in the land of Canaan. Now therefore, we pray thee, let thy servants dwell in the land of Goshen' " [Gen. 47:4].

"Few in number": as it is said: "Thy fathers went down into Egypt with threescore and ten persons; and now the Lord thy God hath made thee as the stars of heaven for multitudes" [Deut. 10:22].

"And he became there a nation": teaching us that the Israelites were distinguishable there. "Great and powerful": as it is said: "And the children of Israel were fruitful, and increased abundantly, and multiplied, and grew exceedingly strong; and the land was

---

implying a command. Others cite the Covenant between the Sections as indicating a compulsion. However, the midrash did not wish to quote again a verse (Gen. 15:13) recorded a few sentences before.

Few in number: In the Sifre our midrash is amplified to read: "Lest you think that he went down into Egypt to assume a royal crown, the Scriptures add, And he sojourned there." Louis Finkelstein (in HTR XXXVI, 1944, 26) observes that the purpose of this passage (greatly antedating the compilation of the Sifre) is to counteract the anti-Semitic interpretation of the Exodus by the Egyptians of the 3rd cent. B. C. E. which identified the ancient Israelites with the Hyksos who invaded Egypt and were later expelled. The comments of the Haggadah and the parallel sources intend to deny any association of the Jews or their ancestors, the Israelites, with an invasion of Egypt "to assume a royal crown." Note also, that a reference to Joseph is avoided, though such reference would be fitting for the Passover celebration. The Haggadah describes Jacob as coming into Egypt with a small family, in order to escape death by starvation.

distinguishable: The midrash emphasizes that the Hebrews did not assimilate in Egypt. According to an ancient tradition, they kept unchanged their names,

וָרָב. כְּמָה שֶׁנֶּאֱמַר: רְבָבָה כְּצֶמַח הַשָּׂדֶה נְתַתִּיךְ וַתִּרְבִּי וַתִּגְדְּלִי וַתָּבֹאִי בַּעֲדִי עֲדָיִים. שָׁדַיִם נָכֹנוּ וּשְׂעָרֵךְ צִמֵּחַ וְאַתְּ עֵרֹם וְעֶרְיָה:

וַיָּרֵעוּ אֹתָנוּ הַמִּצְרִים וַיְעַנּוּנוּ. וַיִּתְּנוּ עָלֵינוּ עֲבֹדָה קָשָׁה:

וַיָּרֵעוּ אֹתָנוּ הַמִּצְרִים. כְּמָה שֶׁנֶּאֱמַר: הָבָה נִתְחַכְּמָה לוֹ. פֶּן־יִרְבֶּה וְהָיָה כִּי־תִקְרֶאנָה מִלְחָמָה וְנוֹסַף גַּם־הוּא עַל־שֹׂנְאֵינוּ וְנִלְחַם־בָּנוּ וְעָלָה מִן־הָאָרֶץ:

וַיְעַנּוּנוּ. כְּמָה שֶׁנֶּאֱמַר: וַיָּשִׂימוּ עָלָיו שָׂרֵי מִסִּים לְמַעַן עַנֹּתוֹ בְּסִבְלֹתָם. וַיִּבֶן עָרֵי מִסְכְּנוֹת לְפַרְעֹה אֶת־פִּתֹם וְאֶת־רַעַמְסֵס:

וַיִּתְּנוּ עָלֵינוּ עֲבֹדָה קָשָׁה. כְּמָה שֶׁנֶּאֱמַר: וַיַּעֲבִדוּ מִצְרַיִם אֶת־בְּנֵי יִשְׂרָאֵל בְּפָרֶךְ:

וַנִּצְעַק אֶל־יְיָ אֱלֹהֵי אֲבֹתֵינוּ. וַיִּשְׁמַע יְיָ אֶת־קֹלֵנוּ וַיַּרְא אֶת־עָנְיֵנוּ וְאֶת־עֲמָלֵנוּ וְאֶת־לַחֲצֵנוּ:

וַנִּצְעַק אֶל־יְיָ אֱלֹהֵי אֲבֹתֵינוּ. כְּמָה שֶׁנֶּאֱמַר: וַיְהִי בַיָּמִים הָרַבִּים הָהֵם וַיָּמָת מֶלֶךְ מִצְרַיִם וַיֵּאָנְחוּ בְנֵי־יִשְׂרָאֵל מִן־הָעֲבֹדָה וַיִּזְעָקוּ. וַתַּעַל שַׁוְעָתָם אֶל־הָאֱלֹהִים מִן־הָעֲבֹדָה:

וַיִּשְׁמַע יְיָ אֶת־קֹלֵנוּ. כְּמָה שֶׁנֶּאֱמַר: וַיִּשְׁמַע אֱלֹהִים אֶת־נַאֲקָתָם. וַיִּזְכֹּר אֱלֹהִים אֶת־בְּרִיתוֹ אֶת־אַבְרָהָם אֶת־יִצְחָק וְאֶת־יַעֲקֹב:

---

their language, and their customs, and some commentators add, their apparel.[5] Finkelstein (HTR XXXI, 304 ff.) maintains that our Haggadah here implies a thinly veiled criticism of the rapid assimilation of the Egyptian Jews during the Second Commonwealth, and an attempt to discourage further immigration into Egypt from the land of Israel.

[5] Cf. Mekhilta on 12:6; Leviticus Rabbah XXXII.4; Numbers Rabbah XX.22; Song of Songs Rabbah IV. Midrash Tehillim 114:1, where Buber (p. 472) indicates additional sources.

filled with them" [Exod. 1:7]. "And populous": as it is said: "I caused thee to increase, even as the growth of the field. And thou didst increase and grow up, and thou camest to excellent beauty: thy breasts were fashioned, and thy hair was grown; yet thou wast naked and bare" [Ezek. 16:7].

"And the Egyptians considered us evil; they afflicted us, and laid upon us hard bondage" [Deut. 26:6].

"And the Egyptians considered us evil": as it is said: "Come let us deal wisely with them, lest they multiply, and it come to pass, that, when there befalleth us any war, they also join themsevles unto our enemies, and fight against us, and get them up out of the land" [Exod. 1:10]. "And afflicted us": as it is said: "Therefore they did set over them taskmasters to afflict them with their burdens. And they built for Pharaoh store-cities, Pithom and Raamses" [Exod. 1:11]. "And laid upon us heavy bondage": as it is said: "And the Egyptians made the children of Israel to serve with rigour" [Exod. 1:13].

"And we cried unto the Lord, the God of our fathers, and the Lord heard our voice, and saw our affliction, and our toil, and our oppression" [Deut. 26:7].

"And we cried unto the Lord, the God of our fathers": as it is written: "And it came to pass in the course of those many days that the king of Egypt died; and the children of Israel sighed by reason of the bondage, and they cried, and their cry came up unto God by reason of the bondage" [Exod. 2:23].

"And the Lord heard our voice": as it is said: "And God heard their groaning, and God remembered His covenant with Abraham, with Isaac and with Jacob" [Exod. 2:24].

And the Egyptians considered us evil: This is how the Haggadah understands the passage; this meaning is also suggested by the quotation from Exodus. The literal translation is: And the Egyptians dealt ill with us.

heavy bondage: According to the Talmud (Sotah 11b), the Egyptians assigned men's work to the women and women's work to the men.

וַיַּרְא אֶת־עָנְיֵנוּ. זוֹ פְּרִישׁוּת דֶּרֶךְ אֶרֶץ. כְּמָה שֶׁנֶּאֱמַר: וַיַּרְא אֱלֹהִים אֶת־בְּנֵי יִשְׂרָאֵל. וַיֵּדַע אֱלֹהִים:

וְאֶת־עֲמָלֵנוּ. אֵלּוּ הַבָּנִים. כְּמָה שֶׁנֶּאֱמַר: כָּל־הַבֵּן הַיִּלּוֹד הַיְאֹרָה תַּשְׁלִיכֻהוּ. וְכָל־הַבַּת תְּחַיּוּן:

וְאֶת־לַחֲצֵנוּ. זֶה הַדְּחַק. כְּמָה שֶׁנֶּאֱמַר: וְגַם־רָאִיתִי אֶת־הַלַּחַץ אֲשֶׁר מִצְרַיִם לֹחֲצִים אֹתָם:

וַיּוֹצִאֵנוּ יְיָ מִמִּצְרַיִם בְּיָד חֲזָקָה וּבִזְרֹעַ נְטוּיָה וּבְמֹרָא גָּדֹל. וּבְאֹתוֹת וּבְמֹפְתִים:

וַיּוֹצִאֵנוּ יְיָ מִמִּצְרַיִם. לֹא־עַל־יְדֵי מַלְאָךְ. וְלֹא־עַל־יְדֵי שָׂרָף. וְלֹא־עַל־יְדֵי שָׁלִיחַ. אֶלָּא הַקָּדוֹשׁ בָּרוּךְ הוּא בִּכְבוֹדוֹ וּבְעַצְמוֹ. שֶׁנֶּאֱמַר: וְעָבַרְתִּי בְאֶרֶץ־מִצְרַיִם בַּלַּיְלָה הַזֶּה וְהִכֵּיתִי כָּל־בְּכוֹר בְּאֶרֶץ מִצְרַיִם מֵאָדָם וְעַד־בְּהֵמָה. וּבְכָל־אֱלֹהֵי מִצְרַיִם אֶעֱשֶׂה שְׁפָטִים אֲנִי יְיָ:

וְעָבַרְתִּי בְאֶרֶץ־מִצְרַיִם בַּלַּיְלָה הַזֶּה. אֲנִי וְלֹא מַלְאָךְ. וְהִכֵּיתִי כָל־בְּכוֹר בְּאֶרֶץ מִצְרַיִם. אֲנִי וְלֹא שָׂרָף. וּבְכָל־אֱלֹהֵי מִצְרַיִם אֶעֱשֶׂה שְׁפָטִים. אֲנִי וְלֹא שָׁלִיחַ. אֲנִי יְיָ. אֲנִי הוּא וְלֹא אַחֵר:

And Pharaoh said: "Every son that is born ye
shall cast into the river . . . ."

44

"And saw our affliction": this is enforced marital continence. As it is said: "And God saw the children of Israel, and God knew" [Exod. 2:25].

"And our travail": this is the sons, as it is said: "Every son that is born ye shall cast into the river, and every daughter ye shall save alive" [Exod. 1:22].

"And our oppression": this is the vexation of which it is said: "Moreover I have seen the oppression wherewith the Egyptians oppress them" [Exod. 3:9].

"And the Lord brought us forth out of Egypt with a mighty hand, and with an outstretched arm, and with great terribleness, and with signs, and with wonders" [Deut. 26:8].

"And the Lord brought us forth out of Egypt": not by the hands of an angel, and not by the hands of a seraph, and not by the hands of a messenger, but the Holy One, blessed be he, himself, in his own glory and in his own person. As it is said: "For I will go through the land of Egypt in that night, and will smite all the first-born in the land of Egypt, both man and beast; and against all the gods of Egypt I will execute judgments: I am the Lord" [Exod. 12:12].

"For I will go through the land of Egypt in that night": I, and not an angel. "I will smite all the first-born in the land of Egypt": I, and not a seraph. "And against all the gods of Egypt I will execute judgments": I, and not a messenger. "I am the Lord": I am He, and no other.

For I will go: This passage duplicates the previous statement. It is omitted in the version of the Haggadah found in the Order of Prayer of Rav Saadia Gaon, in Maimonides' Code, and the Yemenite ritual.

The midrash continues with a series of explanations which point out the concrete meaning of the scriptural phrases. Corresponding passages are quoted from the Scriptures, as proof and illustration.

בְּיָד חֲזָקָה. זוֹ הַדֶּבֶר. כְּמָה שֶׁנֶּאֱמַר: הִנֵּה יַד־יְיָ הוֹיָה בְּמִקְנְךָ אֲשֶׁר בַּשָּׂדֶה בַּסּוּסִים בַּחֲמֹרִים בַּגְּמַלִּים בַּבָּקָר וּבַצֹּאן. דֶּבֶר כָּבֵד מְאֹד:

וּבִזְרֹעַ נְטוּיָה. זוֹ הַחֶרֶב. כְּמָה שֶׁנֶּאֱמַר: וְחַרְבּוֹ שְׁלוּפָה בְּיָדוֹ נְטוּיָה עַל־יְרוּשָׁלָיִם:

וּבְמֹרָא גָדֹל. זוֹ גִלּוּי שְׁכִינָה. כְּמָה שֶׁנֶּאֱמַר: אוֹ הֲנִסָּה אֱלֹהִים לָבוֹא לָקַחַת לוֹ גוֹי מִקֶּרֶב גּוֹי בְּמַסֹּת בְּאֹתֹת וּבְמוֹפְתִים וּבְמִלְחָמָה וּבְיָד חֲזָקָה וּבִזְרוֹעַ נְטוּיָה וּבְמוֹרָאִים גְּדֹלִים. כְּכֹל אֲשֶׁר־עָשָׂה לָכֶם יְיָ אֱלֹהֵיכֶם בְּמִצְרַיִם לְעֵינֶיךָ:

וּבְאֹתוֹת. זֶה הַמַּטֶּה. כְּמָה שֶׁנֶּאֱמַר: וְאֶת־הַמַּטֶּה הַזֶּה תִּקַּח בְּיָדֶךָ. אֲשֶׁר תַּעֲשֶׂה־בּוֹ אֶת־הָאֹתֹת:

וּבְמֹפְתִים. זֶה הַדָּם. כְּמָה שֶׁנֶּאֱמַר: וְנָתַתִּי מוֹפְתִים בַּשָּׁמַיִם וּבָאָרֶץ. דָּם וָאֵשׁ וְתִימְרוֹת עָשָׁן:

דָּבָר אַחֵר. בְּיָד חֲזָקָה שְׁתַּיִם. וּבִזְרֹעַ נְטוּיָה שְׁתַּיִם. וּבְמֹרָא גָדֹל שְׁתַּיִם. וּבְאֹתוֹת שְׁתַּיִם. וּבְמֹפְתִים שְׁתַּיִם:

And with great terribleness: The midrash reads or interprets the word *mora*, "terribleness," as *mareh*, "appearance," the revelation of the Divine Presence.

Finkelstein (HTR XXXI, 309 ff.) maintains that the midrash here is trying to popularize the belief that the appearance of the Deity in visible form is possible. This controversial doctrine was a major source of dispute between the Sadducees and the Pharisees; the Sadducees held that such an appearance of the Deity was possible, while the Pharisees held that it was not. Consequently this midrash must have been accepted before the Pharisaic order attained sufficient power to

"With a mighty hand": this is the blight, as it is said: "Behold, the hand of the Lord is upon thy cattle which are in the field, upon the horses, upon the asses, upon the camels, upon the herds, and upon the flocks; there shall be a very grievous blight" [Exod. 9:3].

"And with an outstretched arm": this is the sword, as it is said: "Having a drawn sword in his hand stretched out over Jerusalem" [I Chron. 21:16].

"And with great terribleness": this is the revelation of the Divine Presence, as it is said: "Or hath God assayed to go and take Him a nation from the midst of another nation, by trials, by signs, and by wonders, and by war, and by a mighty hand, and by an outstretched arm, and by great terrors, according to all that the Lord your God did for you in Egypt before thine eyes?" [Deut. 4:34].

"And with signs": this is the rod of Moses, as it is said: "And thou shalt take in thy hand this rod, wherewith thou shalt do the signs" [Exod. 4:17].

"And with wonders": this is the blood, as it is said: "And I will show wonders in the heavens and in the earth, blood, and fire, and pillars of smoke" [Joel 3:3].

Another explanation is: "A mighty hand" makes two, "an outstretched arm" makes two, "and with great terribleness" makes two, "and with signs" makes two, "and with wonders" makes two.

---

prevent the inclusion of a doctrine contrary to its beliefs in the liturgy, i. e., in pre-Maccabean times.

Another explanation: Since the first three phrases each contain two words in the Hebrew, they are each assigned the numerical value of two; equally the two final phrases, which, though single words, are in plural form. The resulting sum of ten alludes to the ten plagues. Hermeneutic devices of this kind are customary in talmudic literature.

אֵלּוּ עֶשֶׂר מַכּוֹת שֶׁהֵבִיא הַקָּדוֹשׁ בָּרוּךְ הוּא עַל־הַמִּצְרִים בְּמִצְרָיִם.
וְאֵלּוּ הֵן:

דָּם. צְפַרְדֵּעַ. כִּנִּים. עָרוֹב. דֶּבֶר. שְׁחִין. בָּרָד. אַרְבֶּה. חֹשֶׁךְ.
מַכַּת־בְּכוֹרוֹת:

רַבִּי יְהוּדָה הָיָה נוֹתֵן בָּהֶם סִמָּנִים.

דְּצַ"ךְ. עַדַ"שׁ. בְּאַחַ"ב:

רַבִּי יוֹסֵי הַגְּלִילִי אוֹמֵר. מִנַּיִן אַתָּה אוֹמֵר שֶׁלָּקוּ הַמִּצְרִים בְּמִצְרַיִם
עֶשֶׂר מַכּוֹת. וְעַל־הַיָּם לָקוּ חֲמִשִּׁים מַכּוֹת: בְּמִצְרַיִם מַה הוּא אוֹמֵר.
וַיֹּאמְרוּ הַחַרְטֻמִּים אֶל־פַּרְעֹה אֶצְבַּע אֱלֹהִים הוּא: וְעַל הַיָּם מַה־דְהוּא
אוֹמֵר. וַיַּרְא יִשְׂרָאֵל אֶת־הַיָּד הַגְּדֹלָה אֲשֶׁר עָשָׂה יְיָ בְּמִצְרַיִם וַיִּרְאוּ
הָעָם אֶת־יְיָ וַיַּאֲמִינוּ בַּיְיָ וּבְמֹשֶׁה עַבְדּוֹ: כַּמָּה לָקוּ בְּאֶצְבַּע. עֶשֶׂר מַכּוֹת.
אֱמֹר מֵעַתָּה בְּמִצְרַיִם לָקוּ עֶשֶׂר מַכּוֹת וְעַל־הַיָּם לָקוּ חֲמִשִּׁים מַכּוֹת:

The Ten Plagues are not counted or classified in the Pentateuch, while their
order in Ps. 78 differs from that in the Exodus story. Philo (Vita Mosis I, 96 ff.)
classifies the plagues according to the following scheme: three were executed by
Aaron, three by Moses, three by God, and one by all three together. The same
classification is to be found in Exodus Rabbah XII.4.

a mnemonic: According to a midrashic tradition (Tanhuma, Exodus, ed.
Buber 13a; Exodus Rabbah VIII.2; V.6), this mnemonic was engraved on Moses'
staff to guide him in the correct order in which the ten plagues were to take place.

The question may arise why a mnemonic sign was necessary for the plagues
well known from the Pentateuch. Solomon Zeitlin (*Jewish Quarterly Review*,
XXXVIII, 1948, p. 455), points out that Psalm 78 mentioned only seven plagues
and Psalm 105 eight and that in neither case is the order the same as given in the
Pentateuch. Furthermore in the Book of Jubilees while ten plagues are recorded
they do not follow the same order as in Exodus. Most likely the various orders as
given in Psalms and the Book of Jubilees were well known. Therefore, Zeitlin
assumes, Rabbi Judah recommended the mnemonic sign to memorize the order as
recorded in the Pentateuch.

It is an ancient custom to pour a little wine from the cup or sprinkle a little
with the finger at the mention of each plague, of the three mnemonic words, and

These make up the ten plagues which the Holy One, blessed be he, brought upon the Egyptians in Egypt, and they are these: blood, frogs, lice, beasts, blight, boils, hail, locusts, darkness, the slaying of the first-born.

Rabbi Judah made a mnemonic [out of the first letters of the Hebrew words for the plagues], thus: DeTZaKh ADaSH BeAHaB.

THE PLAGUES

Rabbi Jose the Galilean said: "Whence do we learn that the Egyptians were smitten with ten plagues in Egypt, and were smitten with fifty plagues on the sea? With regard to Egypt, what does it say? 'Then the magicians said unto Pharaoh: This is the finger of God' [Exod. 8:15]. And with regard to the sea, what does it say? 'And Israel saw the great hand which the Lord laid upon the Egyptians and the people feared the Lord; and they believed in the Lord, and in His servant Moses' [Exod. 14:31]. With how many were they smitten where it says one finger? Ten plagues. We can say from this that in Egypt they were smitten with ten plagues while at sea they were smitten with fifty plagues."

---

the three wonders in the verse from Joel. Originally this deliberate waste was intended to avert ill-fortune by safeguarding against immoderate rejoicing. This practice — in itself alien to the spirit of Judaism — has interesting parallels in universal folklore. In recent times an attempt has been made by S. R. Hirsch and Eduard Baneth to interpret this custom as a symbolic tempering of the joy of the evening, in order to show sympathy for the misfortune of the Egyptians.

THE PLAGUES

Two supplements to the midrash follow. The first is a series of three tannaitic midrashim on Exod. 14:31 which speak in hyperboles of the Ten Plagues,[6] while the second is an ancient hymn of thanksgiving.

In the first supplement a ratio of one to five is arrived at in a comparison of the blows which the Egyptians suffered at home with those they suffered at sea. This seemingly naive "computation" is intended to extol the miracle.

[6] Mekhilta on 14:30. Mekhilta de Rabbi Simeon ben Yohai (ed. Hoffmann), p. 55. See also Exodus Rabbah V.14; XXIII.9; Midrash Tehillim on 78:49, (ed. Buber), p. 354. Another tradition is preserved in Avot V.4.

בני ישראל בונים ערי מסכנות לפרעה.

TOP: The enslavement of the Children of Israel. Trieste, Italy, 1864 (JTSAL).
BOTTOM: The Children of Israel building cities for Pharaoh.
Trieste, Italy, 1864 (JTSAL).

The ten plagues. Venice, Italy, 1695 (JTSAL).

רַבִּי אֱלִיעֶזֶר אוֹמֵר. מִנַּיִן שֶׁכָּל־מַכָּה וּמַכָּה שֶׁהֵבִיא הַקָּדוֹשׁ בָּרוּךְ הוּא עַל־הַמִּצְרִים בְּמִצְרַיִם הָיְתָה שֶׁל אַרְבַּע מַכּוֹת. שֶׁנֶּאֱמַר: יְשַׁלַּח־ בָּם חֲרוֹן אַפּוֹ עֶבְרָה וָזַעַם וְצָרָה מִשְׁלַחַת מַלְאֲכֵי רָעִים: עֶבְרָה אַחַת. וָזַעַם שְׁתַּיִם. וְצָרָה שָׁלשׁ. מִשְׁלַחַת מַלְאֲכֵי רָעִים אַרְבַּע: אֱמוֹר מֵעַתָּה. בְּמִצְרַיִם לָקוּ אַרְבָּעִים מַכּוֹת וְעַל־הַיָּם לָקוּ מָאתַיִם מַכּוֹת:

רַבִּי עֲקִיבָא אוֹמֵר. מִנַּיִן שֶׁכָּל־מַכָּה וּמַכָּה שֶׁהֵבִיא הַקָּדוֹשׁ בָּרוּךְ הוּא עַל־הַמִּצְרִים בְּמִצְרַיִם הָיְתָה שֶׁל חָמֵשׁ מַכּוֹת. שֶׁנֶּאֱמַר: יְשַׁלַּח־בָּם חֲרוֹן אַפּוֹ עֶבְרָה וָזַעַם וְצָרָה מִשְׁלַחַת מַלְאֲכֵי רָעִים: חֲרוֹן אַפּוֹ אַחַת. עֶבְרָה שְׁתַּיִם. וָזַעַם שָׁלשׁ. וְצָרָה אַרְבַּע. מִשְׁלַחַת מַלְאֲכֵי רָעִים חָמֵשׁ: אֱמוֹר מֵעַתָּה. בְּמִצְרַיִם לָקוּ חֲמִשִּׁים מַכּוֹת וְעַל־הַיָּם לָקוּ חֲמִשִּׁים וּמָאתַיִם מַכּוֹת:

כַּמָּה מַעֲלוֹת טוֹבוֹת לַמָּקוֹם עָלֵינוּ:

אִלּוּ הוֹצִיאָנוּ מִמִּצְרַיִם

וְלֹא עָשָׂה בָהֶם שְׁפָטִים   דַּיֵּנוּ:

אִלּוּ עָשָׂה בָהֶם שְׁפָטִים

וְלֹא עָשָׂה דִין בֵּאלֹהֵיהֶם   דַּיֵּנוּ:

Rabbi Akiba's elaboration of Rabbi Eliezer's commentary gives the impression of being a primitive statement. Presumably it was not meant seriously but was rather an attempt to reduce Rabbi Eliezer's account to an absurdity by carrying his method to an extreme.

WE SHOULD HAVE BEEN CONTENT

The second supplement, an ancient thanksgiving hymn on God's mercies from the time of the exodus from Egypt until Israel's entrance into Canaan. It consists of two parts: a poem and a prose epilogue which summarizes the poem. The hymn is very ancient; presumably it originated in the 2nd cent. B. C. E.

Rabbi Eliezer said: "Whence do we learn that each and every plague that the Holy One, blessed be he, brought upon the Egyptians in Egypt was the same as four plagues? For it is said: 'He sent forth upon them the fierceness of His anger, wrath, and indignation, and trouble, a legation of messengers of evil' [cf. Ps. 78:49]. 'Wrath' makes one, 'indignation' two, 'trouble' three, 'a legation of messengers of evil' four. You can say from this that they were smitten with forty plagues in Egypt and at sea they were smitten with two hundred plagues."

Rabbi Akiba said: "Whence do we learn that each and every plague that the Holy One, blessed be he, brought upon the Egyptians in Egypt was the same as five plagues? For it is said: "He sent forth upon them the fierceness of His anger, wrath, and indignation, and trouble, a legation of messengers of evil" [*ibid.*]. 'The fierceness of His anger' makes one, 'wrath' two, 'indignation' three, 'trouble' four, 'a legation of messengers of evil' five. You can say from this that they were smitten with fifty plagues in Egypt, and at sea they were smitten with two hundred and fifty plagues."

WE SHOULD HAVE BEEN CONTENT

How many are the claims of the Omnipresent upon our thankfulness!
Had He taken us out of Egypt,
> but not executed judgments on them,
>> We should have been content!
Had He executed judgments on them,
> but not upon their gods,
>> We should have been content!

It is a litany, a liturgical form common in ancient Jewish prayers, e. g., *avinu malkenu, al het,* and some penitential prayers (*selihot*) and Hoshana chants. In its present state it contains fourteen strophes and mentions fifteen beneficent acts. Fifteen, according to the Kabbalists, is the numerical value of one of the names of God (YH, spelled Yah); the number fifteen is also symbolic of the fifteen steps in the Temple of Jerusalem. Some of the strophes are differently worded repetitions of others (cf. strophes 2 and 4; 6 and 7; 9 and 10; 12–13).

אִלּוּ עָשָׂה דִין בֵּאלֹהֵיהֶם

וְלֹא הָרַג בְּכוֹרֵיהֶם

דַּיֵּנוּ:

אִלּוּ הָרַג בְּכוֹרֵיהֶם

וְלֹא נָתַן לָנוּ אֶת־מָמוֹנָם

דַּיֵּנוּ:

אִלּוּ נָתַן לָנוּ אֶת־מָמוֹנָם

וְלֹא קָרַע לָנוּ אֶת־הַיָּם

דַּיֵּנוּ:

אִלּוּ קָרַע לָנוּ אֶת־הַיָּם

וְלֹא הֶעֱבִירָנוּ בְתוֹכוֹ בֶּחָרָבָה

דַּיֵּנוּ:

אִלּוּ הֶעֱבִירָנוּ בְתוֹכוֹ בֶּחָרָבָה

וְלֹא שִׁקַּע צָרֵינוּ בְּתוֹכוֹ

דַּיֵּנוּ:

אִלּוּ שִׁקַּע צָרֵינוּ בְּתוֹכוֹ

וְלֹא סִפֵּק צָרְכֵּנוּ בַּמִּדְבָּר אַרְבָּעִים שָׁנָה

דַּיֵּנוּ:

אִלּוּ סִפֵּק צָרְכֵּנוּ בַּמִּדְבָּר אַרְבָּעִים שָׁנָה

וְלֹא הֶאֱכִילָנוּ אֶת־הַמָּן

דַּיֵּנוּ:

אִלּוּ הֶאֱכִילָנוּ אֶת־הַמָּן

וְלֹא נָתַן לָנוּ אֶת־הַשַּׁבָּת

דַּיֵּנוּ:

אִלּוּ נָתַן לָנוּ אֶת־הַשַּׁבָּת

וְלֹא קֵרְבָנוּ לִפְנֵי הַר סִינַי

דַּיֵּנוּ:

אִלּוּ קֵרְבָנוּ לִפְנֵי הַר סִינַי

וְלֹא נָתַן לָנוּ אֶת־הַתּוֹרָה

דַּיֵּנוּ:

אִלּוּ נָתַן לָנוּ אֶת־הַתּוֹרָה

וְלֹא הִכְנִיסָנוּ לְאֶרֶץ יִשְׂרָאֵל

דַּיֵּנוּ:

אִלּוּ הִכְנִיסָנוּ לְאֶרֶץ יִשְׂרָאֵל

וְלֹא בָנָה לָנוּ אֶת־בֵּית הַבְּחִירָה

דַּיֵּנוּ:

Had He executed judgments on their gods,
    but not slain their first-born,
        We should have been content!

Had He slain their first-born,
    but not given us their substance,
        We should have been content!

Had He given us their substance,
    but not torn the Sea apart for us,
        We should have been content!

Had He torn the Sea apart for us,
    but not brought us through it dry,
        We should have been content!

Had He brought us through it dry,
    but not sunk our oppressors in the midst of it,
        We should have been content!

Had He sunk our oppressors in the midst of it,
    but not satisfied our needs in the desert for forty years,
        We should have been content!

Had He satisfied our needs in the desert for forty years,
    but not fed us manna,
        We should have been content!

Had He fed us manna,
    but not given us the Sabbath,
        We should have been content!

Had He given us the Sabbath,
    but not brought us to Mount Sinai,
        We should have been content!

Had He brought us to Mount Sinai,
    but not given us the Torah,
        We should have been content!

Had He given us the Torah,
    but not brought us into the Land of Israel,
        We should have been content!

Had He brought us into the Land of Israel,
    but not built us the House of his choosing,
        We should have been content!

עַל־אַחַת כַּמָּה וְכַמָּה טוֹבָה כְפוּלָה וּמְכֻפֶּלֶת לַמָּקוֹם עָלֵינוּ. שֶׁהוֹצִיאָנוּ
מִמִּצְרַיִם. וְעָשָׂה בָהֶם שְׁפָטִים. וְעָשָׂה דִין בֵּאלֹהֵיהֶם. וְהָרַג בְּכוֹרֵיהֶם.
וְנָתַן לָנוּ אֶת־מָמוֹנָם. וְקָרַע לָנוּ אֶת־הַיָּם. וְהֶעֱבִירָנוּ בְתוֹכוֹ בֶּחָרָבָה.
וְשִׁקַּע צָרֵינוּ בְּתוֹכוֹ. וְסִפֵּק צָרְכֵּנוּ בַּמִּדְבָּר אַרְבָּעִים שָׁנָה. וְהֶאֱכִילָנוּ
אֶת־הַמָּן. וְנָתַן לָנוּ אֶת־הַשַּׁבָּת. וְקֵרְבָנוּ לִפְנֵי הַר סִינַי. וְנָתַן לָנוּ אֶת־
הַתּוֹרָה. וְהִכְנִיסָנוּ לְאֶרֶץ יִשְׂרָאֵל. וּבָנָה לָנוּ אֶת־בֵּית הַבְּחִירָה. לְכַפֵּר
עַל־כָּל־עֲוֹנוֹתֵינוּ:

רַבָּן גַּמְלִיאֵל הָיָה אוֹמֵר: כָּל־שֶׁלֹּא אָמַר שְׁלֹשָׁה דְבָרִים אֵלוּ בַּפֶּסַח
לֹא יָצָא יְדֵי חוֹבָתוֹ: וְאֵלוּ הֵן.

פֶּסַח.

מַצָּה.

וּמָרוֹר:

פֶּסַח שֶׁהָיוּ אֲבוֹתֵינוּ אוֹכְלִים בִּזְמַן שֶׁבֵּית הַמִּקְדָּשׁ הָיָה קַיָּם עַל־שׁוּם
מָה. עַל־שׁוּם שֶׁפָּסַח הַקָּדוֹשׁ בָּרוּךְ הוּא.עַל־בָּתֵּי אֲבוֹתֵינוּ בְּמִצְרָיִם.
שֶׁנֶּאֱמַר: וַאֲמַרְתֶּם זֶבַח־פֶּסַח הוּא לַיְיָ אֲשֶׁר פָּסַח עַל־בָּתֵּי בְנֵי־יִשְׂרָאֵל
בְּמִצְרַיִם בְּנָגְפּוֹ אֶת־מִצְרַיִם וְאֶת־בָּתֵּינוּ הִצִּיל. וַיִּקֹּד הָעָם וַיִּשְׁתַּחֲווּ:

PASSOVER SACRIFICE,
UNLEAVENED BREAD AND BITTER HERBS

The original text, as found in the Mishnah (Pesahim X. 5), reads simply: "The Passover Sacrifice (is offered) because the Holy One, blessed be he, passed over the houses of our fathers in Egypt; unleavened bread (is eaten) because our fathers were redeemed from Egypt; the bitter herb (is eaten) because the Egyptians embittered the lives of our fathers in Egypt." This brief formula was expanded in later generations, and the section regarding the Passover Sacrifice was changed to the past tense after the destruction of the Temple.

It is customary to lift up the unleavened bread and bitter herbs when describing their significance, but not the shankbone, which symbolizes the Passover Sacrifice. Sacrifices were forbidden after the destruction of the Temple, and any gesture

Then how much more, doubled and redoubled, is the claim the Omnipresent has upon our thankfulness! For he did take us out of Egypt, and execute judgments on them, and judgments on their gods, and slay their first-born, and give us their substance, and tear the Sea apart for us, and bring us through it dry, and sink our oppressors in the midst of it, and satisfy our needs in the desert for forty years, and feed us manna, and give us the Sabbath, and bring us to Mount Sinai, and give us the Torah, and bring us into the Land of Israel, and build us the House of his choosing to atone for all our sins.

PASSOVER SACRIFICE, UNLEAVENED BREAD, AND BITTER HERBS

Rabban Gamaliel used to say: "Whoever does not make mention of the following three things on Passover has not fulfilled his obligation: namely, the Passover Sacrifice, unleavened bread, and bitter herbs."

The Passover Sacrifice which our fathers used to eat at the time when the Holy Temple still stood — what was the reason for it? Because the Holy One, blessed be he, passed over the houses of our fathers in Egypt.

As it is said: "It is the sacrifice of the Lord's passover, for that He passed over the houses of the children of Israel in Egypt, when He smote the Egyptians, and delivered our houses. And the people bowed the head and worshipped" [Exod. 12:27].

---

which might lend the shankbone more than a character of a remembrance of sacrifice was avoided.

mention: Here meaning "clarify" or "explain." Rabban Gamaliel is cautioning against a mechanical performance of the Seder rites, without an awareness of their significance. His prescription is unusual, however, for it is not customary to accompany the performance of religious rites with such explanations (except in a few cases where the rite is rabbinic rather than biblical in origin, e. g., the kindling of the Hanukkah candles). His statement should therefore be read in the light of the biblical injunction that the father explain the meaning of the Passover rites to his children. In fact, this selection constitutes the only direct reply to some of the Four Questions.

The master of the house lifts up the matzot, showing them to
the celebrants.

מַצָּה זוֹ שֶׁאָנוּ אוֹכְלִים עַל־שׁוּם מָה. עַל־שׁוּם שֶׁלֹּא הִסְפִּיק בְּצֵקָם

שֶׁל־אֲבוֹתֵינוּ לְהַחֲמִיץ עַד־שֶׁנִּגְלָה עֲלֵיהֶם מֶלֶךְ מַלְכֵי הַמְּלָכִים

הַקָּדוֹשׁ בָּרוּךְ הוּא וּגְאָלָם.

שֶׁנֶּאֱמַר: וַיֹּאפוּ אֶת־הַבָּצֵק אֲשֶׁר הוֹצִיאוּ מִמִּצְרַיִם עֻגֹת מַצּוֹת כִּי לֹא

חָמֵץ. כִּי־גֹרְשׁוּ מִמִּצְרַיִם וְלֹא יָכְלוּ לְהִתְמַהְמֵהַּ וְגַם־צֵדָה לֹא־עָשׂוּ

לָהֶם:

The master of the house lifts up the bitter herbs, showing them
to the celebrants.

מָרוֹר זֶה שֶׁאָנוּ אוֹכְלִים עַל־שׁוּם מָה. עַל־שׁוּם שֶׁמֵּרְרוּ הַמִּצְרִים

אֶת־חַיֵּי אֲבוֹתֵינוּ בְּמִצְרָיִם.

שֶׁנֶּאֱמַר: וַיְמָרְרוּ אֶת־חַיֵּיהֶם בַּעֲבֹדָה קָשָׁה בְּחֹמֶר וּבִלְבֵנִים וּבְכָל־

עֲבֹדָה בַּשָּׂדֶה. אֵת כָּל־עֲבֹדָתָם אֲשֶׁר־עָבְדוּ בָהֶם בְּפָרֶךְ:

בְּכָל־דּוֹר וָדוֹר חַיָּב אָדָם לִרְאוֹת אֶת־עַצְמוֹ כְּאִלּוּ הוּא יָצָא מִמִּצְרָיִם.

שֶׁנֶּאֱמַר: וְהִגַּדְתָּ לְבִנְךָ בַּיּוֹם הַהוּא לֵאמֹר. בַּעֲבוּר זֶה עָשָׂה יְיָ לִי

בְּצֵאתִי מִמִּצְרָיִם:

לֹא אֶת־אֲבוֹתֵינוּ בִּלְבַד גָּאַל הַקָּדוֹשׁ בָּרוּךְ הוּא. אֶלָּא אַף אוֹתָנוּ גָּאַל

עִמָּהֶם.

שֶׁנֶּאֱמַר: וְאוֹתָנוּ הוֹצִיא מִשָּׁם. לְמַעַן הָבִיא אֹתָנוּ לָתֶת לָנוּ אֶת־הָאָרֶץ

אֲשֶׁר נִשְׁבַּע לַאֲבֹתֵינוּ:

The master of the house lifts up the matzot, showing them to the celebrants.

This matzah which we eat, what is the reason for it? Because the dough of our fathers had not yet leavened when the King over all kings, the Holy One, blessed be he, revealed himself to them and redeemed them.

As it is said: "And they baked unleavened cakes of the dough which they brought forth out of Egypt, for it was not leavened; because they were thrust out of Egypt, and could not tarry, neither had they prepared for themselves any victual" [Exod. 12:39].

The master of the house lifts up the bitter herbs, showing them to the celebrants.

These bitter herbs we eat, what is the reason for them? Because the Egyptians made the lives of our forefathers bitter in Egypt.

As it is said: "And they made their lives bitter with hard service, in mortar and in brick, and in all manner of service in the field; in all their service, wherein they made them serve with rigour" [Exod. 1:14].

IN EVERY GENERATION

In every generation let each man look on himself as if *he* came forth out of Egypt.

As it is said: "And thou shalt tell thy son in that day, saying: It is because of that which the Lord did for me when I came forth out of Egypt" [Exod. 13:8].

It was not only our fathers that the Holy One, blessed be he, redeemed, but us as well did he redeem along with them.

As it is said: "And He brought us out from thence, that He might bring us in, to give us the land which He swore unto our fathers" [Deut. 6:23].

IN EVERY GENERATION

The text is based on Mishnah Pesahim X. 5. A passage of central importance in the Haggadah: Exodus and redemption are not to be taken as happenings in long bygone days, but as a personal experience.

The participants lift up their cups of wine and say:

The master of the Seder
lifts up his cup of wine

לְפִיכָךְ אֲנַחְנוּ חַיָּבִים לְהוֹדוֹת, לְהַלֵּל, לְשַׁבֵּחַ, לְפָאֵר, לְרוֹמֵם, לְהַדֵּר, לְבָרֵךְ, לְעַלֵּה, וּלְקַלֵּס, לְמִי שֶׁעָשָׂה לַאֲבוֹתֵינוּ וְלָנוּ אֶת־כָּל־הַנִּסִּים הָאֵלוּ. הוֹצִיאָנוּ מֵעַבְדוּת לְחֵרוּת. מִיָּגוֹן לְשִׂמְחָה. מֵאֵבֶל לְיוֹם טוֹב. וּמֵאֲפֵלָה לְאוֹר גָּדוֹל. וּמִשִּׁעְבּוּד לִגְאֻלָּה. וְנֹאמַר לְפָנָיו וְשִׁירָה חֲדָשָׁה. הַלְלוּיָהּ:

The cups are put back on the table.

הַלְלוּיָהּ

הַלְלוּ עַבְדֵי יְיָ. הַלְלוּ אֶת־שֵׁם יְיָ:

יְהִי שֵׁם יְיָ מְבֹרָךְ מֵעַתָּה וְעַד עוֹלָם:

מִמִּזְרַח־שֶׁמֶשׁ עַד־מְבוֹאוֹ מְהֻלָּל שֵׁם יְיָ:

רָם עַל־כָּל־גּוֹיִם יְיָ עַל הַשָּׁמַיִם כְּבוֹדוֹ:

מִי כַּיְיָ אֱלֹהֵינוּ הַמַּגְבִּיהִי לָשָׁבֶת:

הַמַּשְׁפִּילִי לִרְאוֹת בַּשָּׁמַיִם וּבָאָרֶץ:

מְקִימִי מֵעָפָר דָּל מֵאַשְׁפֹּת יָרִים אֶבְיוֹן:

לְהוֹשִׁיבִי עִם־נְדִיבִים עִם נְדִיבֵי עַמּוֹ:

מוֹשִׁיבִי עֲקֶרֶת הַבַּיִת אֵם־הַבָּנִים שְׂמֵחָה הַלְלוּיָהּ:

The participants lift up their cups of wine and say:

Therefore, we are bound to thank, praise, laud, glorify, exalt, honor, bless, extol, and adore Him who performed all these miracles for our fathers and for us. He has brought us forth from slavery to freedom, from sorrow to joy, from mourning to holiday, from darkness to great light, and from bondage to redemption. Let us then recite before him a new song: Hallelujah.

The cups are put back on the table.

THE HALLEL: FIRST PART

Hallelujah. / Praise, O ye servants of the Lord, / Praise the name of the Lord.

Blessed be the name of the Lord / From this time forth and for ever.

From the rising of the sun unto the going down thereof / The Lord's name is to be praised.

The Lord is high above all nations, / His glory is above the heavens.

Who is like unto the Lord our God, / That is enthroned on high,

That looketh down low / Upon heaven and upon the earth?

Who raiseth up the poor out of the dust, / And lifteth up the needy out of the dunghill;

That He may set him with princes, / Even with the princes of His people.

Who maketh the barren woman to dwell in her house / As a joyful mother of children. / Hallelujah.

The Hallel: First Part

The Hallel: A series of psalms (113–118) which the Levites chanted in the Temple during the offering of the paschal lamb (Mishnah Pesahim V. 7). Only the first two Hallel psalms (113 and 114) are recited before the Seder meal. Psalm 113:1 calls upon the "servants of the Lord" to praise him; this rabbinical tradition interprets to mean: "Servants of the Lord, but not servants of Pharaoh" (Megillah 14a).

בְּצֵאת יִשְׂרָאֵל מִמִּצְרָיִם בֵּית יַעֲקֹב מֵעַם לֹעֵז:

הָיְתָה יְהוּדָה לְקָדְשׁוֹ יִשְׂרָאֵל מַמְשְׁלוֹתָיו:

הַיָּם רָאָה וַיָּנֹס הַיַּרְדֵּן יִסֹּב לְאָחוֹר:

הֶהָרִים רָקְדוּ כְאֵילִים גְּבָעוֹת כִּבְנֵי־צֹאן:

מַה־לְּךָ הַיָּם כִּי תָנוּס הַיַּרְדֵּן תִּסֹּב לְאָחוֹר:

הֶהָרִים תִּרְקְדוּ כְאֵילִים גְּבָעוֹת כִּבְנֵי־צֹאן:

מִלִּפְנֵי אָדוֹן חוּלִי אָרֶץ מִלִּפְנֵי אֱלוֹהַּ יַעֲקֹב:

הַהֹפְכִי הַצּוּר אֲגַם־מָיִם חַלָּמִישׁ לְמַעְיְנוֹ־מָיִם:

"When Israel came forth out of Egypt . . . ."

The participants lift up their cups of wine and say:

בָּרוּךְ אַתָּה יְיָ אֱלֹהֵינוּ מֶלֶךְ הָעוֹלָם. אֲשֶׁר גְּאָלָנוּ וְגָאַל אֶת־אֲבוֹתֵינוּ

מִמִּצְרַיִם וְהִגִּיעָנוּ הַלַּיְלָה הַזֶּה לֶאֱכָל־בּוֹ מַצָּה וּמָרוֹר. כֵּן יְיָ אֱלֹהֵינוּ

וֵאלֹהֵי אֲבוֹתֵינוּ הַגִּיעֵנוּ לְמוֹעֲדִים וְלִרְגָלִים אֲחֵרִים הַבָּאִים לִקְרָאתֵנוּ

לְשָׁלוֹם שְׂמֵחִים בְּבִנְיַן עִירֶךָ וְשָׂשִׂים בַּעֲבוֹדָתֶךָ. וְנֹאכַל שָׁם מִן

62

When Israel came forth out of Egypt, / The house of Jacob from a people of strange language;

Judah became His sanctuary, / Israel His dominion.

The sea saw it, and fled; / The Jordan turned backward.

The mountains skipped like rams, / The hills like young sheep.

What aileth thee, O thou sea, that thou fleest? / Thou Jordan, that thou turnest backward?

Ye mountains, that ye skip like rams; / Ye hills, like young sheep?

Tremble, thou earth, at the presence of the Lord, / At the presence of the God of Jacob;

Who turned the rock into a pool of water, / The flint into a fountain of waters.

REDEMPTION

The participants lift up their cups of wine and say:

Blessed art thou, O Lord, our God, king of the universe, who redeemed us and who redeemed our fathers from Egypt, and has brought us to this night, to eat thereon unleavened bread and bitter herbs. So, O Lord our God and God of our fathers, bring us to other festivals and holy days that come toward us in peace, happy in the building of thy city and joyous in thy service. And there may we

---

REDEMPTION

The first sentence of this benediction was prescribed by Rabbi Tarfon, the rest, including the sequence on the rebuilding of Jersualem, by Rabbi Akiba (Mishnah Pesahim X. 6). Rabbi Akiba, in the year 132, participated in the rebellion led by Bar Kokhba against the Roman domination of the land of Israel. The last part of the benediction reflects his hope for the liberation of the land of Israel; a hope the fufillment of which we witness in our own days.[7]

[7] *min ha-pesahim umin ha-zevahim* seems to be the correct version, regardless of whether *zevahim* be taken in a general or a technical sense (as the *hagigah* of the evening). The wording of the variant זבחים ומן הפסחים מן [=במשניות] 'במש, commonly interpreted as במ'ש [במוצאי שבת], gave rise to the mistaken practice of changing the version on Saturday evening, a practice already opposed by Rabbi Jacob Emden.

הַזְּבָחִים וּמִן הַפְּסָחִים אֲשֶׁר יַגִּיעַ דָּמָם עַל־קִיר מִזְבַּחֲךָ לְרָצוֹן.

וְנוֹדֶה לְךָ ‏[שִׁיר חָדָשׁ] עַל־גְּאֻלָּתֵנוּ ‏[וְעַל פְּדוּת נַפְשֵׁנוּ]: בָּרוּךְ אַתָּה יְיָ.

גָּאַל יִשְׂרָאֵל:

בָּרוּךְ אַתָּה יְיָ אֱלֹהֵינוּ מֶלֶךְ הָעוֹלָם. בּוֹרֵא פְּרִי הַגָּפֶן:

The second cup of wine is drunk in a reclining position.

רחץ

The participants wash their hands and say the following benediction:

בָּרוּךְ אַתָּה יְיָ אֱלֹהֵינוּ מֶלֶךְ הָעוֹלָם. אֲשֶׁר קִדְּשָׁנוּ בְּמִצְוֹתָיו וְצִוָּנוּ עַל

נְטִילַת יָדָיִם:

מוציא

The master of the Seder breaks pieces from the upper and middle wafers and distributes them; the following benedictions are recited:

בָּרוּךְ אַתָּה יְיָ אֱלֹהֵינוּ מֶלֶךְ הָעוֹלָם. הַמּוֹצִיא לֶחֶם מִן הָאָרֶץ:

מצה

בָּרוּךְ אַתָּה יְיָ אֱלֹהֵינוּ מֶלֶךְ הָעוֹלָם. אֲשֶׁר קִדְּשָׁנוּ בְּמִצְוֹתָיו וְצִוָּנוּ עַל

אֲכִילַת מַצָּה:

The matzah is eaten in a reclining position.

eat of the sacrifices and the paschal offerings, whose blood will come unto the walls of thy altar for acceptance. Then shall we give thanks to thee with a new song, for our redemption and the liberation of our soul. Blessed art thou, O Lord, Redeemer of Israel.

Blessed art thou, O Lord our God, king of the universe, creator of the fruit of the vine.

The second cup of wine is drunk in a reclining position.

THE MEAL

The participants wash their hands and say the following benediction:

Blessed art thou, O Lord our God, king of the universe, who sanctified us with his commandments, and commanded us concerning the washing of hands.

The master of the Seder breaks pieces from the upper and middle wafers and distributes them; the following benedictions are recited:

Blessed art thou, O Lord our God, king of the universe, who brings forth bread from the earth.

Blessed art thou, O Lord our God, king of the universe, who sanctified us with his commandments, and commanded us concerning the eating of unleavened bread.

The matzah is eaten in a reclining position.

THE MEAL

The benediction on bread is recited over the two whole wafers of matzah. The second benediction, that on unleavened bread is recited over the fragment of the middle matzah.

According to usage, each participant eats of the *afikoman* a piece at least the "size of an olive" (roughly half an egg). The eating of the *afikoman* is an essential

מָרוֹר

The master of the Seder dips some bitter herbs in the *haroset* and offers a piece to each participant. The following benediction is said before eating the bitter herbs:

בָּרוּךְ אַתָּה יְיָ אֱלֹהֵינוּ מֶלֶךְ הָעוֹלָם. אֲשֶׁר קִדְּשָׁנוּ בְּמִצְוֹתָיו וְצִוָּנוּ עַל אֲכִילַת מָרוֹר:

כּוֹרֵךְ

The master of the Seder breaks the bottom matzah, puts some bitter herb sandwich-fashion between two pieces of matzah.

The following is recited before eating:

זֵכֶר לְמִקְדָּשׁ כְּהִלֵּל:

כֵּן עָשָׂה הִלֵּל בִּזְמַן שֶׁבֵּית הַמִּקְדָּשׁ הָיָה קַיָם. הָיָה כּוֹרֵךְ [פֶּסַח] מַצָּה וּמָרוֹר וְאוֹכֵל בְּיַחַד. לְקַיֵּם מַה שֶּׁנֶּאֱמַר: עַל־מַצּוֹת וּמְרוֹרִים יֹאכְלֻהוּ:

The Seder platter is removed.

שֻׁלְחָן עוֹרֵךְ

At this point the Seder meal is eaten.

צָפוּן

After the meal the Seder platter is again placed on the table. The matzah which has been set aside for *afikoman* is distributed among the Seder company.

Family seder in the nineteenth century. Trieste, Italy, 1864 (JTSAL).

The master of the Seder dips some bitter herbs in the *haroset*
and offers a piece to each participant. The following benediction
is spoken before eating the bitter herbs:

Blessed art thou, O Lord our God, king of the universe, who
sanctified us with his commandments, and commanded us concerning
the eating of bitter herbs.

The master of the Seder breaks the bottom matzah, puts some
bitter herb sandwich-fashion between two pieces of matzah.
The following is recited before eating:

In memory of the Temple, according to the custom of Hillel.
Thus did Hillel when the Holy Temple still stood: he used to
combine unleavened bread and bitter herbs and eat them together,
to fulfil that which is said: "They shall eat it with unleavened bread
and bitter herbs" [Num. 9:11].

The Seder platter is removed.
At this point the Seder meal is eaten.

After the meal the Seder platter is again placed on the table. The
matzah which has been set aside for *afikoman* is distributed among
the Seder company.

---

part of our Seder service, for it is a reminder of the paschal lamb. If it is omitted
by an oversight and the omission noted only after the Grace, one is bound to wash
again, pronounce the blessings over bread, eat the *afikoman*, and repeat the Grace.
In Sephardic and Oriental rituals the following formula is pronounced before the
eating of the *afikoman*: זֵכֶר לְקָרְבַּן פֶּסַח הַנֶּאֱכָל עַל הַשּׂוֹבַע *In memory of
the Passover sacrifice, eaten after one is sated.*

After the *afikoman* no more food may be partaken and — besides the two
prescribed cups of wine — only water may be drunk that night.

בָּרֵךְ

Before Grace the third cup is filled. If three or more males are present, the following introductory phrases are recited. If ten or more are present, the words in brackets are also recited.

The master of the Seder:

רַבּוֹתַי נְבָרֵךְ:

The participants:

יְהִי שֵׁם יְיָ מְבֹרָךְ מֵעַתָּה וְעַד־עוֹלָם:

The master of the Seder:

בִּרְשׁוּת רַבּוֹתַי נְבָרֵךְ [אֱלֹהֵינוּ] שֶׁאָכַלְנוּ מִשֶּׁלּוֹ:

The participants:

בָּרוּךְ [אֱלֹהֵינוּ] שֶׁאָכַלְנוּ מִשֶּׁלּוֹ וּבְטוּבוֹ חָיִינוּ:

All:

בָּרוּךְ אַתָּה יְיָ אֱלֹהֵינוּ מֶלֶךְ הָעוֹלָם הַזָּן אֶת־הָעוֹלָם כֻּלּוֹ בְּטוּבוֹ בְּחֵן בְּחֶסֶד וּבְרַחֲמִים הוּא נוֹתֵן לֶחֶם לְכָל־בָּשָׂר כִּי לְעוֹלָם חַסְדּוֹ:

וּבְטוּבוֹ הַגָּדוֹל תָּמִיד לֹא־חָסַר לָנוּ וְאַל יֶחְסַר לָנוּ מָזוֹן לְעוֹלָם וָעֶד. בַּעֲבוּר שְׁמוֹ הַגָּדוֹל.

כִּי הוּא זָן וּמְפַרְנֵס לַכֹּל וּמֵטִיב לַכֹּל וּמֵכִין מָזוֹן לְכָל בְּרִיּוֹתָיו אֲשֶׁר בָּרָא.

בָּרוּךְ אַתָּה יְיָ הַזָּן אֶת־הַכֹּל:

GRACE

The Grace at the Seder is not different from that which follows all meals, except that on this occasion the diners are enjoined to drink the cup of wine otherwise optional. The main part of the Grace contains four benedictions, the first three very ancient and known long before the destruction of the Temple, the fourth a supplement by the sages of Jabneh after the rebellion of Bar Kokhba (Berakhot

Before Grace the third cup is filled. If three or more men are present, the following introductory phrases are recited. If ten or more are present, the words in brackets are also recited. (Grace is customarily preceded by the singing of Psalm 126.)

The master of the Seder:

Gentlemen, let us say the blessing.

The participants:

May the Name of the Lord be blessed from now unto eternity.

The master of the Seder:

Let us bless Him [our God] of whose food we have eaten.

The participants:

Blessed be He [our God] of whose food we have eaten and through whose goodness we live.

All:

Blessed art thou, O Lord our God, king of the world, who feeds the entire world in his goodness, with grace, lovingkindness, and compassion. He gives bread to all flesh, for his mercy is forever.

And through his great goodness, food has never failed us, and may it never fail us, for his great Name's sake.

For he feeds and sustains all, and does good unto all, and prepares food for all his creatures which he did create.

Blessed art thou, O Lord, who feeds all.

48b). The first benediction expresses thanks for the food, and the second thanks for the Land of Israel; the third is a petition for the restoration of the Holy City; the fourth is a thanksgiving to Him "who is good and does good," and ends with the hope "may he not let us lack of all that is good." The rest of the Grace contains later additions.

נוֹדֶה לְּךָ יְיָ אֱלֹהֵינוּ עַל שֶׁהִנְחַלְתָּ לַאֲבוֹתֵינוּ אֶרֶץ חֶמְדָּה טוֹבָה וּרְחָבָה.

וְעַל שֶׁהוֹצֵאתָנוּ יְיָ אֱלֹהֵינוּ מֵאֶרֶץ מִצְרַיִם וּפְדִיתָנוּ מִבֵּית עֲבָדִים.

וְעַל בְּרִיתְךָ שֶׁחָתַמְתָּ בִּבְשָׂרֵנוּ וְעַל תּוֹרָתְךָ שֶׁלִּמַּדְתָּנוּ וְעַל חֻקֶּיךָ שֶׁהוֹדַעְתָּנוּ.

וְעַל חַיִּים חֵן וָחֶסֶד שֶׁחוֹנַנְתָּנוּ.

וְעַל אֲכִילַת מָזוֹן שָׁאַתָּה זָן וּמְפַרְנֵס אוֹתָנוּ תָּמִיד בְּכָל־יוֹם וּבְכָל־עֵת וּבְכָל־שָׁעָה:

וְעַל הַכֹּל יְיָ אֱלֹהֵינוּ אֲנַחְנוּ מוֹדִים לָךְ וּמְבָרְכִים אוֹתָךְ יִתְבָּרַךְ שִׁמְךָ בְּפִי כָל־חַי תָּמִיד לְעוֹלָם וָעֶד:

כַּכָּתוּב וְאָכַלְתָּ וְשָׂבָעְתָּ וּבֵרַכְתָּ אֶת־יְיָ אֱלֹהֶיךָ עַל־הָאָרֶץ הַטֹּבָה אֲשֶׁר נָתַן־לָךְ.

בָּרוּךְ אַתָּה יְיָ עַל־הָאָרֶץ וְעַל־הַמָּזוֹן:

רַחֵם יְיָ אֱלֹהֵינוּ עַל־יִשְׂרָאֵל עַמֶּךָ וְעַל־יְרוּשָׁלַיִם עִירֶךָ וְעַל־צִיּוֹן מִשְׁכַּן כְּבוֹדֶךָ וְעַל־מַלְכוּת בֵּית דָּוִד מְשִׁיחֶךָ וְעַל־הַבַּיִת הַגָּדוֹל וְהַקָּדוֹשׁ שֶׁנִּקְרָא שִׁמְךָ עָלָיו:

אֱלֹהֵינוּ אָבִינוּ רְעֵנוּ זוּנֵנוּ פַּרְנְסֵנוּ וְכַלְכְּלֵנוּ וְהַרְוִיחֵנוּ וְהַרְוַח־לָנוּ יְיָ אֱלֹהֵינוּ מְהֵרָה מִכָּל־צָרוֹתֵינוּ:

וְנָא אַל־תַּצְרִיכֵנוּ יְיָ אֱלֹהֵינוּ לֹא לִידֵי מַתְּנַת בָּשָׂר וָדָם וְלֹא לִידֵי הַלְוָאָתָם. כִּי־אִם לְיָדְךָ הַמְּלֵאָה הַפְּתוּחָה הַקְּדוֹשָׁה וְהָרְחָבָה שֶׁלֹּא נֵבוֹשׁ וְלֹא נִכָּלֵם לְעוֹלָם וָעֶד:

On Sabbath the following paragraph is added:

רְצֵה וְהַחֲלִיצֵנוּ יְיָ אֱלֹהֵינוּ בְּמִצְוֹתֶיךָ וּבְמִצְוַת יוֹם הַשְּׁבִיעִי הַשַּׁבָּת הַגָּדוֹל וְהַקָּדוֹשׁ הַזֶּה כִּי יוֹם זֶה גָּדוֹל וְקָדוֹשׁ הוּא לְפָנֶיךָ לִשְׁבָּת־בּוֹ וְלָנוּחַ בּוֹ בְּאַהֲבָה כְּמִצְוַת רְצוֹנֶךָ:

Let us give thanks to thee, O Lord our God, because thou hast
given our fathers to inherit a pleasant land, goodly and broad,
and because thou hast brought us forth, O Lord our God, from the
land of Egypt, and redeemed us out of the house of slaves;
and for thy covenant which thou hast sealed in our flesh; and for
thy Torah which thou hast taught us; and for thy laws which
thou hast informed us;
and for the life, grace, and mercy which thou hast graciously given
us;
and for the eating of the food with which thou feedest and sustainest
us continually, every day, at all times and at every hour.

And for all this, O Lord our God, we give thanks to thee and give
blessing to thee; blessed be thy name in the mouth of each
living thing forever, continually.
As it is written: "And thou shalt eat and be satisfied, and bless the
Lord thy God for the good land which He hath given thee"
[Deut. 8:10].
Blessed art thou, O Lord, for the land and for the food.

Take pity, O Lord our God, on Israel, thy folk, and on Jerusalem,
thy city, and on Zion, the habitation of thy glory, and on the
kingdom of the House of David, thine anointed, and upon the
great and holy House over which thy name is called.
Our God, our Father, shepherd us, feed us, maintain us, sustain us,
and ease us. Ease us, O Lord our God, speedily from all our
troubles.
And let us not be needing, O Lord our God, gifts at the hands of
flesh and blood, or their loans, but only at thy hand, that is
full and open, holy and broad, so that we be never ashamed or
disgraced at all.

On Sabbath the following paragraph is added:

[Be it thy pleasure and strengthen us, O Lord our God, by thy
commandments, and by the commandment of the seventh day,
this Sabbath great and sacred; for this day is great and sacred
before thee, that we may halt and rest thereon, in love, according
to the command of thy will.

בִּרְצוֹנְךָ הָנִיחַ לָנוּ יְיָ אֱלֹהֵינוּ שֶׁלֹּא תְהִי צָרָה וְיָגוֹן וַאֲנָחָה בְּיוֹם מְנוּחָתֵנוּ.

וְהַרְאֵנוּ יְיָ אֱלֹהֵינוּ בְּנֶחָמַת צִיּוֹן עִירֶךָ וּבְבִנְיַן יְרוּשָׁלַיִם עִיר קָדְשֶׁךָ. כִּי אַתָּה הוּא בַּעַל הַיְשׁוּעוֹת וּבַעַל הַנֶּחָמוֹת:]

אֱלֹהֵינוּ וֵאלֹהֵי אֲבוֹתֵינוּ. יַעֲלֶה וְיָבֹא וְיַגִּיעַ וְיֵרָאֶה וְיֵרָצֶה וְיִשָּׁמַע וְיִפָּקֵד וְיִזָּכֵר זִכְרוֹנֵנוּ וּפִקְדּוֹנֵנוּ. וְזִכְרוֹן אֲבוֹתֵינוּ. וְזִכְרוֹן מָשִׁיחַ בֶּן דָּוִד עַבְדֶּךָ. וְזִכְרוֹן יְרוּשָׁלַיִם עִיר קָדְשֶׁךָ. וְזִכְרוֹן כָּל־עַמְּךָ בֵּית יִשְׂרָאֵל לְפָנֶיךָ. לִפְלֵטָה לְטוֹבָה לְחֵן וּלְחֶסֶד וּלְרַחֲמִים לְחַיִּים וּלְשָׁלוֹם בְּיוֹם חַג הַמַּצּוֹת הַזֶּה.

זָכְרֵנוּ יְיָ אֱלֹהֵינוּ בּוֹ לְטוֹבָה. וּפָקְדֵנוּ בוֹ לִבְרָכָה. וְהוֹשִׁיעֵנוּ בוֹ לְחַיִּים.

וּבִדְבַר יְשׁוּעָה וְרַחֲמִים חוּס וְחָנֵּנוּ. וְרַחֵם עָלֵינוּ וְהוֹשִׁיעֵנוּ. כִּי אֵלֶיךָ עֵינֵינוּ. כִּי אֵל מֶלֶךְ חַנּוּן וְרַחוּם אָתָּה:

וּבְנֵה יְרוּשָׁלַיִם עִיר הַקֹּדֶשׁ בִּמְהֵרָה בְיָמֵינוּ: בָּרוּךְ אַתָּה יְיָ. בּוֹנֵה בְרַחֲמָיו יְרוּשָׁלָיִם. אָמֵן:

בָּרוּךְ אַתָּה יְיָ אֱלֹהֵינוּ מֶלֶךְ הָעוֹלָם. הָאֵל אָבִינוּ מַלְכֵּנוּ אַדִּירֵנוּ בּוֹרְאֵנוּ גֹּאֲלֵנוּ יוֹצְרֵנוּ קְדוֹשֵׁנוּ קְדוֹשׁ יַעֲקֹב רוֹעֵנוּ רוֹעֵה יִשְׂרָאֵל הַמֶּלֶךְ הַטּוֹב וְהַמֵּטִיב לַכֹּל שֶׁבְּכָל יוֹם וָיוֹם הוּא הֵטִיב הוּא מֵטִיב הוּא יֵיטִיב לָנוּ: הוּא גְמָלָנוּ הוּא גוֹמְלֵנוּ הוּא יִגְמְלֵנוּ לָעַד לְחֵן לְחֶסֶד וּלְרַחֲמִים וּלְרֶוַח הַצָּלָה וְהַצְלָחָה בְּרָכָה וִישׁוּעָה נֶחָמָה פַּרְנָסָה וְכַלְכָּלָה וְרַחֲמִים וְחַיִּים וְשָׁלוֹם וְכָל־טוֹב וּמִכָּל־טוּב אַל יְחַסְּרֵנוּ:

And at thy will, give us rest, O Lord our God, that there be no
   sorrow, grief, or sighing on the day of our rest;
and let us see, O Lord our God, the consolation of Zion, thy city,
   and the building of Jerusalem, thy sacred city. For thou art
   the master of salvations and the master of consolations.]

Our God and God of our fathers, may there rise, and come,
and come unto, be seen, accepted, heard, recollected and remembered,
the remembrance of us and the recollection of us, and the remembrance of our fathers, and the remembrance of the Messiah, son of
David, thy servant, and the remembrance of Jerusalem, thy holy
city, and the remembrance of all thy people, the house of Israel.
May their remembrance come before thee, for rescue, goodness,
grace, mercy, and compassion, for life and for peace, on this the
Festival of Unleavened Bread.

Remember us, O Lord our God, thereon for good, and recollect us
   thereon for a blessing, and save us thereon to live.
And with word of salvation and compassion spare us and be gracious
   with us; have compassion on us and save us — for to thee are
   our eyes, for thou art a God gracious and compassionate.

And build Jerusalem, the sacred city, speedily in our days.
Blessed art thou, O Lord, who builds in his compassion Jerusalem.
Amen.

Blessed art thou, O Lord our God, king of the universe, O God,
our Father, our King, our Mighty One, our Creator, our Redeemer,
our Maker, our Sacred One, the Sacred One of Jacob, our Shepherd,
the Shepherd of Israel, the King, who is good and does good to all,
he who every day, did, does, and will do good to us. He has favored,
he favors, he will favor us forever: for grace, for mercy, and for
compassion and for ease, rescue, and success, blessing and salvation,
consolation, maintenance and sustenance, and compassion and life
and peace, and all that is good; may he not let us lack of all that is
good.

הָרַחֲמָן הוּא יִמְלוֹךְ עָלֵינוּ לְעוֹלָם וָעֶד:

הָרַחֲמָן הוּא יִתְבָּרַךְ בַּשָּׁמַיִם וּבָאָרֶץ:

הָרַחֲמָן הוּא יִשְׁתַּבַּח לְדוֹר דּוֹרִים וְיִתְפָּאַר־בָּנוּ לָנֶצַח נְצָחִים וְיִתְהַדַּר־בָּנוּ לָעַד וּלְעוֹלְמֵי עוֹלָמִים:

הָרַחֲמָן הוּא יְפַרְנְסֵנוּ בְּכָבוֹד:

הָרַחֲמָן הוּא יִשְׁבּוֹר עֻלֵּנוּ מֵעַל צַוָּארֵנוּ וְהוּא יוֹלִיכֵנוּ קוֹמְמִיּוּת לְאַרְצֵנוּ:

הָרַחֲמָן הוּא יִשְׁלַח בְּרָכָה מְרֻבָּה בַּבַּיִת הַזֶּה וְעַל שֻׁלְחָן זֶה שֶׁאָכַלְנוּ עָלָיו:

הָרַחֲמָן הוּא יִשְׁלַח־לָנוּ אֶת־אֵלִיָּהוּ הַנָּבִיא זָכוּר לַטּוֹב וִיבַשֶּׂר־לָנוּ בְּשׂוֹרוֹת טוֹבוֹת יְשׁוּעוֹת וְנֶחָמוֹת:

הָרַחֲמָן הוּא יְבָרֵךְ אֶת (אָבִי מוֹרִי) בַּעַל הַבַּיִת הַזֶּה וְאֶת (אִמִּי מוֹרָתִי) בַּעֲלַת הַבַּיִת הַזֶּה אוֹתָם וְאֶת־בֵּיתָם וְאֶת־זַרְעָם וְאֶת־כָּל־אֲשֶׁר לָהֶם (אוֹתִי וְאֶת אִשְׁתִּי וְאֶת זַרְעִי וְאֶת כָּל אֲשֶׁר לִי) (וְכָל הַמְּסֻבִּין כַּאן) אוֹתָנוּ וְאֶת־כָּל־אֲשֶׁר לָנוּ כְּמוֹ שֶׁנִּתְבָּרְכוּ אֲבוֹתֵינוּ אַבְרָהָם יִצְחָק וְיַעֲקֹב בַּכֹּל מִכֹּל כֹּל. כֵּן יְבָרֵךְ אוֹתָנוּ כֻּלָּנוּ יַחַד בִּבְרָכָה שְׁלֵמָה וְנֹאמַר אָמֵן:

בַּמָּרוֹם יְלַמְּדוּ עֲלֵיהֶם וְעָלֵינוּ זְכוּת שֶׁתְּהִי לְמִשְׁמֶרֶת שָׁלוֹם. וְנִשָּׂא בְרָכָה מֵאֵת יְיָ וּצְדָקָה מֵאֱלֹהֵי יִשְׁעֵנוּ: וְנִמְצָא־חֵן וְשֵׂכֶל טוֹב בְּעֵינֵי אֱלֹהִים וְאָדָם:

On Sabbath add the following paragraph:

[הָרַחֲמָן הוּא יַנְחִילֵנוּ יוֹם שֶׁכֻּלּוֹ שַׁבָּת וּמְנוּחָה לְחַיֵּי הָעוֹלָמִים:]

הָרַחֲמָן הוּא יַנְחִילֵנוּ יוֹם שֶׁכֻּלּוֹ טוֹב:

הָרַחֲמָן הוּא יְזַכֵּנוּ לִימוֹת הַמָּשִׁיחַ וּלְחַיֵּי הָעוֹלָם הַבָּא:

74

The Compassionate One — may he reign over us for ever and ever.

The Compassionate One — may he be blessed in the heavens and on the earth.

The Compassionate One — may he be lauded throughout all the generations, and glory in us for ever and for all eternity, and be honored in us for ever and ever.

The Compassionate One — may he sustain us with honor.

The Compassionate One — may he break our yoke from off our neck and may he lead us upright to our land.

The Compassionate One — may he send much blessing to us in this house and to this table from which we have eaten.

The Compassionate One — may he send Elijah, the prophet (may he be remembered for good), to us, that he may bring us good tidings of salvations and consolations.

The Compassionate One — may he bless [my father and teacher] the master of this house, and [my mother and teacher] the mistress of this house, and their household and their seed and all they have [myself, and my wife, and my children, and all I have] [and all at this table], us and all we have. As our fathers, Abraham, Isaac, and Jacob were blessed in all, of all, all — so bless thou us altogether with a perfect blessing, and let us say, Amen.

On high, may the merits of their case and ours be pleaded successfully, that it may become a guardian of peace. And may we bear away a blessing from the Lord, and righteousness from the God of our salvation. May we find grace and good favor in the eyes of God and man.

On Sabbath add the following paragraph:

[The Compassionate One — may he cause us to inherit that day which is all Sabbath and repose, in the everlasting life.]

The Compassionate One — may he cause us to inherit a day that is all good.

The Compassionate One — may he find us worthy of the days of the Messiah and of the life of the world to come.

מִגְדּוֹל יְשׁוּעוֹת מַלְכּוֹ וְעֹשֶׂה חֶסֶד לִמְשִׁיחוֹ לְדָוִד וּלְזַרְעוֹ עַד־עוֹלָם.

עֹשֶׂה שָׁלוֹם בִּמְרוֹמָיו הוּא יַעֲשֶׂה שָׁלוֹם עָלֵינוּ וְעַל־כָּל־יִשְׂרָאֵל וְאִמְרוּ

אָמֵן:

יְראוּ אֶת־יְיָ קְדֹשָׁיו כִּי אֵין מַחְסוֹר לִירֵאָיו:

כְּפִירִים רָשׁוּ וְרָעֵבוּ וְדֹרְשֵׁי יְיָ לֹא־יַחְסְרוּ כָל־טוֹב:

הוֹדוּ לַיְיָ כִּי־טוֹב כִּי לְעוֹלָם חַסְדּוֹ:

פּוֹתֵחַ אֶת־יָדֶךָ וּמַשְׂבִּיעַ לְכָל־חַי רָצוֹן:

בָּרוּךְ הַגֶּבֶר אֲשֶׁר יִבְטַח בַּיְיָ וְהָיָה יְיָ מִבְטַחוֹ:

נַעַר הָיִיתִי גַּם־זָקַנְתִּי וְלֹא־רָאִיתִי צַדִּיק נֶעֱזָב וְזַרְעוֹ מְבַקֶּשׁ לָחֶם:

יְיָ עֹז לְעַמּוֹ יִתֵּן יְיָ יְבָרֵךְ אֶת־עַמּוֹ בַשָּׁלוֹם:

The participants lift up their cups of wine and say:

בָּרוּךְ אַתָּה יְיָ אֱלֹהֵינוּ מֶלֶךְ הָעוֹלָם. בּוֹרֵא פְּרִי הַגָּפֶן:

The third cup of wine is drunk while in a reclining position.

The door is opened and the following verses are recited:

שְׁפֹךְ חֲמָתְךָ אֶל־הַגּוֹיִם אֲשֶׁר לֹא־יְדָעוּךָ וְעַל־מַמְלָכוֹת אֲשֶׁר בְּשִׁמְךָ

לֹא קָרָאוּ: כִּי אָכַל אֶת־יַעֲקֹב וְאֶת־נָוֵהוּ הֵשַׁמּוּ: שְׁפָךְ־עֲלֵיהֶם זַעְמֶךָ

וַחֲרוֹן אַפְּךָ יַשִּׂיגֵם: תִּרְדֹּף בְּאַף וְתַשְׁמִידֵם מִתַּחַת שְׁמֵי יְיָ:

The door is closed.

POUR OUT THY WRATH

The custom of reciting these verses after the Grace originated under the
stress of persecution in the Middle Ages (possibly during the period of the Cru-
sades). Some commentators believed that they referred to the heathen that had

"A tower of salvation is He to His king; / And showeth mercy to His anointed, / To David and to his seed, for evermore" (II Sam. 22:51). He who makes peace in his high places, he shall make peace for us and for all Israel, and say ye, Amen.

"O fear the Lord, ye His holy ones; / For there is no want to them that fear him" [Ps. 34:10].
"The young lions do lack and suffer hunger; / But they that seek the Lord want not any good thing" [Ps. 34:11].
"O give thanks unto the Lord, for He is good, / For His mercy endureth for ever" [Ps. 118:1].
"Thou openest Thy hand, / And satisfiest every living thing with favour" [Ps. 145:16].
"Blessed is the man that trusteth in the Lord, / and whose trust the Lord is" [Jer. 17:7].
"I have been young, and now am old; / Yet have I not seen the righteous forsaken, / Nor his seed begging bread" [Ps. 37:25].
"The Lord will give strength unto His people; the Lord will bless His people with peace" [Ps. 29:11].

The participants lift up their cup of wine and say:

Blessed art Thou, O Lord our God, king of the universe, creator of the fruit of the vine.

The third cup of wine is drunk while in a reclining position.

POUR OUT THY WRATH
The door is opened and the following verses are recited:

"Pour out Thy wrath upon the nations that know Thee not, / And upon the kingdoms that call not upon Thy name. / For they have devoured Jacob, / And laid waste his habitation" [Ps. 79:6–7]. "Pour out Thine indignation upon them, / And let the fierceness of Thine anger overtake them" [Ps. 69:25]. "Thou wilt pursue them in anger, and destroy them / From under the heavens of the Lord" [Lam. 3:66].

The door is closed.

---

destroyed the Temple; others excluded the adherents of monotheistic faiths.[8]

[8] Eliezer Ashkenazi in the commentary to the Haggadah in his *Maase Adonai* (Venice 1583). See Jacob Katz, *Exclusiveness and Tolerance*, New York 1962, p. 166.

וינער ה' את מצריים בתוך חים ⋮ וּבני ישראל חלכו כיבשה בתרך חים

The crossing of the Red Sea. Amsterdam, Netherlands, 1695 (JTSAL).

The Messiah enters Jerusalem, heralded by
the prophet Elijah. Mantua, Italy, 1560 (JTSAL).

The fourth cup is filled and the Hallel recital concluded.

לֹא לָנוּ יְיָ לֹא לָנוּ כִּי לְשִׁמְךָ תֵּן כָּבוֹד עַל־חַסְדְּךָ עַל־אֲמִתֶּךָ:

לָמָּה יֹאמְרוּ הַגּוֹיִם אַיֵּה־נָא אֱלֹהֵיהֶם:

וֵאלֹהֵינוּ בַשָּׁמָיִם כֹּל אֲשֶׁר־חָפֵץ עָשָׂה:

עֲצַבֵּיהֶם כֶּסֶף וְזָהָב מַעֲשֵׂה יְדֵי אָדָם:

פֶּה־לָהֶם וְלֹא יְדַבֵּרוּ עֵינַיִם לָהֶם וְלֹא יִרְאוּ:

אָזְנַיִם לָהֶם וְלֹא יִשְׁמָעוּ אַף לָהֶם וְלֹא יְרִיחוּן:

יְדֵיהֶם וְלֹא יְמִישׁוּן רַגְלֵיהֶם וְלֹא יְהַלֵּכוּ לֹא יֶהְגּוּ בִּגְרוֹנָם:

כְּמוֹהֶם יִהְיוּ עֹשֵׂיהֶם כֹּל אֲשֶׁר־בֹּטֵחַ בָּהֶם:

יִשְׂרָאֵל בְּטַח בַּיְיָ עֶזְרָם וּמָגִנָּם הוּא:

בֵּית אַהֲרֹן בִּטְחוּ בַיְיָ עֶזְרָם וּמָגִנָּם הוּא:

יִרְאֵי יְיָ בִּטְחוּ בַיְיָ עֶזְרָם וּמָגִנָּם הוּא:

יְיָ זְכָרָנוּ יְבָרֵךְ יְבָרֵךְ אֶת־בֵּית יִשְׂרָאֵל יְבָרֵךְ אֶת־בֵּית אַהֲרֹן:

יְבָרֵךְ יִרְאֵי יְיָ הַקְּטַנִּים עִם הַגְּדֹלִים:

יֹסֵף יְיָ עֲלֵיכֶם עֲלֵיכֶם וְעַל־בְּנֵיכֶם:

בְּרוּכִים אַתֶּם לַיְיָ עֹשֵׂה שָׁמַיִם וָאָרֶץ:

הַשָּׁמַיִם שָׁמַיִם לַיְיָ וְהָאָרֶץ נָתַן לִבְנֵי אָדָם:

לֹא הַמֵּתִים יְהַלְלוּ־יָהּ וְלֹא כָּל־יֹרְדֵי דוּמָה:

וַאֲנַחְנוּ נְבָרֵךְ יָהּ מֵעַתָּה וְעַד־עוֹלָם הַלְלוּיָהּ:

King David

80

The fourth cup is filled and the Hallel recital concluded.

Not unto us, O Lord, not unto us, / But unto Thy name give glory, / For Thy mercy, and for Thy truth's sake.

Wherefore should the nations say: / 'Where is now their God?'

But our God is in the heavens; / Whatsoever pleased Him He hath done.

Their idols are silver and gold, / The work of men's hands.

They have mouths, but they speak not; / Eyes have they, but they see not;

They have ears, but they hear not; / Noses have they, but they smell not;

They have hands, but they handle not; / Feet have they, but they walk not; / Neither speak they with their throat.

They that make them shall be like unto them; / Yea, every one that trusteth in them.

O Israel, trust thou in the Lord! / He is their help and their shield!

O house of Aaron, trust ye in the Lord! / He is their help and their shield!

Ye that fear the Lord, trust in the Lord! / He is their help and their shield.

The Lord hath been mindful of us, He will bless — / He will bless the house of Israel; / He will bless the house of Aaron.

He will bless them that fear the Lord, / Both small and great.

The Lord increase you more and more, / You and your children.

Blessed be ye of the Lord, / Who made heaven and earth.

The heavens are the heavens of the Lord; / But the earth hath He given to the children of men.

The dead praise not the Lord, / Neither any that go down into silence;

But we will bless the Lord / From this time forth and for ever. / Hallelujah.

אָהַבְתִּי כִּי־יִשְׁמַע יְיָ אֶת־קוֹלִי תַּחֲנוּנָי:

כִּי־הִטָּה אָזְנוֹ לִי וּבְיָמַי אֶקְרָא:

אֲפָפוּנִי חֶבְלֵי־מָוֶת וּמְצָרֵי שְׁאוֹל מְצָאוּנִי צָרָה וְיָגוֹן אֶמְצָא:

וּבְשֵׁם יְיָ אֶקְרָא אָנָּה יְיָ מַלְּטָה נַפְשִׁי:

חַנּוּן יְיָ וְצַדִּיק וֵאלֹהֵינוּ מְרַחֵם:

שֹׁמֵר פְּתָאיִם יְיָ דַּלּוֹתִי וְלִי יְהוֹשִׁיעַ:

שׁוּבִי נַפְשִׁי לִמְנוּחָיְכִי כִּי־יְיָ גָּמַל עָלָיְכִי:

כִּי חִלַּצְתָּ נַפְשִׁי מִמָּוֶת אֶת־עֵינִי מִן־דִּמְעָה אֶת־רַגְלִי מִדֶּחִי:

אֶתְהַלֵּךְ לִפְנֵי יְיָ בְּאַרְצוֹת הַחַיִּים:

הֶאֱמַנְתִּי כִּי אֲדַבֵּר אֲנִי עָנִיתִי מְאֹד:

אֲנִי אָמַרְתִּי בְחָפְזִי כָּל־הָאָדָם כֹּזֵב:

מָה־אָשִׁיב לַיְיָ כָּל־תַּגְמוּלוֹהִי עָלָי:

כּוֹס־יְשׁוּעוֹת אֶשָּׂא וּבְשֵׁם יְיָ אֶקְרָא:

נְדָרַי לַיְיָ אֲשַׁלֵּם נֶגְדָה־נָּא לְכָל־עַמּוֹ:

יָקָר בְּעֵינֵי יְיָ הַמָּוְתָה לַחֲסִידָיו:

אָנָּה יְיָ כִּי־אֲנִי עַבְדֶּךָ אֲנִי־עַבְדְּךָ בֶּן־אֲמָתֶךָ פִּתַּחְתָּ לְמוֹסֵרָי:

לְךָ־אֶזְבַּח זֶבַח תּוֹדָה וּבְשֵׁם יְיָ אֶקְרָא:

נְדָרַי לַיְיָ אֲשַׁלֵּם נֶגְדָה־נָּא לְכָל־עַמּוֹ:

בְּחַצְרוֹת בֵּית יְיָ בְּתוֹכֵכִי יְרוּשָׁלָיִם הַלְלוּיָהּ:

הַלְלוּ אֶת־יְיָ כָּל־גּוֹיִם שַׁבְּחוּהוּ כָּל־הָאֻמִּים:

כִּי גָבַר עָלֵינוּ חַסְדּוֹ וֶאֱמֶת־יְיָ לְעוֹלָם הַלְלוּיָהּ:

I love that the Lord should hear / My voice and my supplications.

Because He hath inclined His ear unto me, / Therefore will I call upon Him all my days.

The cords of death compassed me, / And the straits of the nether-world got hold upon me; / I found trouble and sorrow.

But I called upon the name of the Lord: / 'I beseech Thee, O Lord, deliver my soul.'

Gracious is the Lord, and righteous; / Yea, our God is compassionate.

The Lord preserveth the simple; / I was brought low, and He saved me.

Return, O my soul, unto thy rest; / For the Lord hath dealt bountifully with thee.

For Thou hast delivered my soul from death, / Mine eyes from tears, / And my feet from stumbling.

I shall walk before the Lord / In the lands of the living.

I trusted even when I spoke: / 'I am greatly afflicted.'

I said in my haste: / 'Men are all a vain hope.'

How can I repay unto the Lord / All His bountiful dealings toward me?

I will lift up the cup of salvation, / And call upon the name of the Lord.

My vows will I pay unto the Lord, / Yea, in the presence of all His people.

Precious in the sight of the Lord / Is the death of His saints.

I beseech Thee, O Lord, for I am thy servant; / I am Thy servant, the son of Thy handmaid; / Thou hast loosed my bands.

I will offer to Thee the sacrifice of thanksgiving, / And will call upon the name of the Lord.

I will pay my vows unto the Lord, / Yea, in the presence of all His people;

In the courts of the Lord's house, / In the midst of thee, O Jerusalem. / Hallelujah.

O praise the Lord, all ye nations; / Laud Him, all ye peoples.

For His mercy is great toward us; / And the truth of the Lord endureth for ever. / Hallelujah.

הוֹדוּ לַיְיָ כִּי־טוֹב   כִּי לְעוֹלָם חַסְדּוֹ:

יֹאמַר־נָא יִשְׂרָאֵל   כִּי לְעוֹלָם חַסְדּוֹ:

יֹאמְרוּ־נָא בֵית־אַהֲרֹן   כִּי לְעוֹלָם חַסְדּוֹ:

יֹאמְרוּ־נָא יִרְאֵי יְיָ   כִּי לְעוֹלָם חַסְדּוֹ:

מִן־הַמֵּצַר קָרָאתִי יָּה עָנָנִי בַמֶּרְחָב יָה:

יְיָ לִי לֹא אִירָא מַה־יַּעֲשֶׂה לִי אָדָם:

יְיָ לִי בְּעֹזְרָי וַאֲנִי אֶרְאֶה בְשֹׂנְאָי:

טוֹב לַחֲסוֹת בַּיְיָ מִבְּטֹחַ בָּאָדָם:

טוֹב לַחֲסוֹת בַּיְיָ מִבְּטֹחַ בִּנְדִיבִים:

כָּל־גּוֹיִם סְבָבוּנִי בְּשֵׁם יְיָ כִּי אֲמִילַם:

סַבּוּנִי גַם־סְבָבוּנִי בְּשֵׁם יְיָ כִּי אֲמִילַם:

סַבּוּנִי כִדְבֹרִים דֹּעֲכוּ כְּאֵשׁ קוֹצִים בְּשֵׁם יְיָ כִּי אֲמִילַם:

דָּחֹה דְחִיתַנִי לִנְפֹּל וַיְיָ עֲזָרָנִי:

עָזִּי וְזִמְרָת יָהּ וַיְהִי־לִי לִישׁוּעָה:

קוֹל רִנָּה וִישׁוּעָה בְּאָהֳלֵי צַדִּיקִים יְמִין יְיָ עֹשָׂה חָיִל:

יְמִין יְיָ רוֹמֵמָה יְמִין יְיָ עֹשָׂה חָיִל:

לֹא־אָמוּת כִּי־אֶחְיֶה וַאֲסַפֵּר מַעֲשֵׂי יָהּ:

יַסֹּר יִסְּרַנִּי יָּהּ וְלַמָּוֶת לֹא נְתָנָנִי:

פִּתְחוּ־לִי שַׁעֲרֵי־צֶדֶק אָבֹא־בָם אוֹדֶה יָהּ:

זֶה־הַשַּׁעַר לַיְיָ צַדִּיקִים יָבֹאוּ בוֹ:

84

'O give thanks unto the Lord, for He is good,
             For His mercy endureth for ever.'
So let Israel now say,
             For His mercy endureth for ever.
So let the house of Aaron now say,
             For His mercy endureth for ever.
So let them now that fear the Lord say,
             For His mercy endureth for ever.

Out of my straits I called upon the Lord; / He answered me with
    great enlargement.
The Lord is for me; I will not fear; / What can man do unto me?
The Lord is for me as my helper; / And I shall gaze upon them
    that hate me.
It is better to take refuge in the Lord / Than to trust in man.
It is better to take refuge in the Lord / Than to trust in princes.
All nations compass me about; / Verily, in the name of the Lord
    I will cut them off.
They compass me about, yea, they compass me about; / Verily,
    in the name of the Lord I will cut them off.
They compass me about like bees; / They are quenched as the fire of
    thorns; / Verily, in the name of the Lord I will cut them off.
Thou didst thrust sore at me that I might fall; / But the Lord helped
    me.
The Lord is my strength and song; / And He is become my
    salvation.
The voice of rejoicing and salvation is in the tents of the righteous;
The right hand of the Lord doeth valiantly.
The right hand of the Lord is exalted; / The right hand of the
    Lord doeth valiantly.
I shall not die, but live, / And declare the works of the Lord.
The Lord hath chastened me sore; / But he hath not given me
    over unto death.
Open to me the gates of righteousness; / I will enter into them,
    I will give thanks unto the Lord.
This is the gate of the Lord; / The righteous shall enter into it.

The following four verses are repeated:

אוֹדְךָ כִּי עֲנִיתָנִי וַתְּהִי־לִי לִישׁוּעָה:

אֶבֶן מָאֲסוּ הַבּוֹנִים הָיְתָה לְרֹאשׁ פִּנָּה:

מֵאֵת יְיָ הָיְתָה זֹּאת הִיא נִפְלָאת בְּעֵינֵינוּ:

זֶה־הַיּוֹם עָשָׂה יְיָ נָגִילָה וְנִשְׂמְחָה בוֹ:

אָנָּא יְיָ הוֹשִׁיעָה נָּא.

אָנָּא יְיָ הוֹשִׁיעָה נָּא:

אָנָּא יְיָ הַצְלִיחָה נָא.

אָנָּא יְיָ הַצְלִיחָה נָא:

"Blessed be he that cometh in
the name of the Lord"

The following verses are repeated:

בָּרוּךְ הַבָּא בְּשֵׁם יְיָ בֵּרַכְנוּכֶם מִבֵּית יְיָ:
אֵל יְיָ וַיָּאֶר לָנוּ אִסְרוּ־חַג בַּעֲבֹתִים עַד־
קַרְנוֹת הַמִּזְבֵּחַ:
אֵלִי אַתָּה וְאוֹדֶךָ אֱלֹהַי אֲרוֹמְמֶךָ:
הוֹדוּ לַיְיָ כִּי־טוֹב כִּי לְעוֹלָם חַסְדּוֹ:

יְהַלְלוּךָ יְיָ אֱלֹהֵינוּ כָּל־מַעֲשֶׂיךָ. וַחֲסִידֶיךָ צַדִּיקִים עוֹשֵׂי רְצוֹנֶךָ. וְכָל־
עַמְּךָ בֵּית־יִשְׂרָאֵל בְּרִנָּה יוֹדוּ וִיבָרְכוּ וִישַׁבְּחוּ וִיפָאֲרוּ וִירוֹמְמוּ וְיַעֲרִיצוּ
וְיַקְדִּישׁוּ וְיַמְלִיכוּ אֶת־שִׁמְךָ מַלְכֵּנוּ: כִּי לְךָ טוֹב לְהוֹדוֹת וּלְשִׁמְךָ נָאֶה
לְזַמֵּר. כִּי מֵעוֹלָם וְעַד־עוֹלָם אַתָּה אֵל:

The following four verses are repeated:

I will give thanks unto Thee, for Thou hast answered me, / And art become my salvation.

The stone which the builders rejected / Is become the chief corner-stone.

This is the Lord's doing; / It is marvellous in our eyes.

This is the day which the Lord hath made; / We will rejoice and be glad in it.

We beseech Thee, O Lord, save now!
We beseech Thee, O Lord, save now!
We beseech Thee, O Lord, make us now to prosper!
We beseech Thee, O Lord, make us now to prosper!

The following verses are repeated:

Blessed be he that cometh in the name of the Lord; / We bless you out of the house of the Lord.

The Lord is God, and hath given us light; / Order the festival procession with boughs, even unto the horns of the altar.

Thou art my God, and I will give thanks unto Thee; / Thou art my God, I will exalt Thee.

O give thanks unto the Lord, for He is good, / For His mercy endureth for ever.

PRAISE THEE

Praise thee, O Lord our God, shall all thy works; and thy pious ones, the righteous who do thy will, and all thy people, the House of Israel, with joyous song, shall give thanks and bless, laud and glorify, and exalt, and fear, sanctify, and declare the kingship of thy Name, our King. For to thee it is good to render thanksgiving, and to thy Name it is becoming to sing, for from eternity to eternity thou art God.

PRAISE THEE

According to the Mishnah (Pesahim X. 7), a "Benediction of Song" follows the conclusion of the Hallel. Of this benediction the Talmud already knew several versions, such as the one before us, and the one recited later, "The breath of every living thing."

הוֹדוּ לַיָי כִּי־טוֹב   כִּי לְעוֹלָם חַסְדּוֹ:

הוֹדוּ לֵאלֹהֵי הָאֱלֹהִים   כִּי לְעוֹלָם חַסְדּוֹ:

הוֹדוּ לַאֲדֹנֵי הָאֲדֹנִים   כִּי לְעוֹלָם חַסְדּוֹ:

לְעֹשֵׂה נִפְלָאוֹת גְּדֹלוֹת לְבַדּוֹ   כִּי לְעוֹלָם חַסְדּוֹ:

לְעֹשֵׂה הַשָּׁמַיִם בִּתְבוּנָה   כִּי לְעוֹלָם חַסְדּוֹ:

לְרֹקַע הָאָרֶץ עַל־הַמָּיִם   כִּי לְעוֹלָם חַסְדּוֹ:

לְעֹשֵׂה אוֹרִים גְּדֹלִים   כִּי לְעוֹלָם חַסְדּוֹ:

אֶת־הַשֶּׁמֶשׁ לְמֶמְשֶׁלֶת בַּיּוֹם   כִּי לְעוֹלָם חַסְדּוֹ:

אֶת־הַיָּרֵחַ וְכוֹכָבִים לְמֶמְשְׁלוֹת בַּלָּיְלָה   כִּי לְעוֹלָם חַסְדּוֹ:

לְמַכֵּה מִצְרַיִם בִּבְכוֹרֵיהֶם   כִּי לְעוֹלָם חַסְדּוֹ:

וַיּוֹצֵא יִשְׂרָאֵל מִתּוֹכָם   כִּי לְעוֹלָם חַסְדּוֹ:

בְּיָד חֲזָקָה וּבִזְרוֹעַ נְטוּיָה   כִּי לְעוֹלָם חַסְדּוֹ:

לְגֹזֵר יַם־סוּף לִגְזָרִים   כִּי לְעוֹלָם חַסְדּוֹ:

וְהֶעֱבִיר יִשְׂרָאֵל בְּתוֹכוֹ   כִּי לְעוֹלָם חַסְדּוֹ:

וְנִעֵר פַּרְעֹה וְחֵילוֹ בְיַם־סוּף   כִּי לְעוֹלָם חַסְדּוֹ:

לְמוֹלִיךְ עַמּוֹ בַּמִּדְבָּר   כִּי לְעוֹלָם חַסְדּוֹ:

לְמַכֵּה מְלָכִים גְּדֹלִים   כִּי לְעוֹלָם חַסְדּוֹ:

The Great Hallel

This is the talmudic term for Psalm 136 (Berakhot 4b; Pesahim 118a; Mishnah Taanit III.9). The Psalm is arranged for antiphonal chanting; the poem is elliptical, the opening line, "O give thanks unto the Lord," being implied before most of the strophes.

O give thanks unto the Lord, for He is good,
>> For His mercy endureth for ever.

O give thanks unto the God of Gods,
>> For His mercy endureth for ever.

O give thanks unto the Lord of lords,
>> For His mercy endureth for ever.

To Him who alone doeth great wonders,
>> For His mercy endureth for ever.

To Him that by understanding made the heavens,
>> For His mercy endureth for ever.

To Him that spread forth the earth above the waters,
>> For His mercy endureth for ever.

To Him that made great lights,
>> For His mercy endureth for ever;

The sun to rule by day,
>> For His mercy endureth for ever;

The moon and stars to rule by night,
>> For His mercy endureth for ever.

To Him that smote Egypt in their first-born,
>> For His mercy endureth for ever;

And brought out Israel from among them,
>> For His mercy endureth for ever;

With a strong hand, and with an outstretched arm,
>> For His mercy endureth for ever.

To Him who divided the Red Sea in sunder,
>> For His mercy endureth for ever;

And made Israel to pass through the midst of it,
>> For His mercy endureth for ever;

But overthrew Pharaoh and his host in the Red Sea,
>> For His mercy endureth for ever.

To Him that led His people through the wilderness,
>> For His mercy endureth for ever.

To Him that smote great kings;
>> For His mercy endureth for ever;

כִּי לְעוֹלָם חַסְדּוֹ: וַיַּהֲרֹג מְלָכִים אַדִּירִים

כִּי לְעוֹלָם חַסְדּוֹ: לְסִיחוֹן מֶלֶךְ הָאֱמֹרִי

כִּי לְעוֹלָם חַסְדּוֹ: וּלְעוֹג מֶלֶךְ הַבָּשָׁן

כִּי לְעוֹלָם חַסְדּוֹ: וְנָתַן אַרְצָם לְנַחֲלָה

כִּי לְעוֹלָם חַסְדּוֹ: נַחֲלָה לְיִשְׂרָאֵל עַבְדּוֹ

כִּי לְעוֹלָם חַסְדּוֹ: שֶׁבְּשִׁפְלֵנוּ זָכַר לָנוּ

כִּי לְעוֹלָם חַסְדּוֹ: וַיִּפְרְקֵנוּ מִצָּרֵינוּ

כִּי לְעוֹלָם חַסְדּוֹ: נֹתֵן לֶחֶם לְכָל־בָּשָׂר

כִּי לְעוֹלָם חַסְדּוֹ: הוֹדוּ לְאֵל הַשָּׁמָיִם

נִשְׁמַת כָּל־חַי תְּבָרֵךְ אֶת־שִׁמְךָ יְיָ אֱלֹהֵינוּ. וְרוּחַ כָּל־בָּשָׂר תְּפָאֵר וּתְרוֹמֵם זִכְרְךָ מַלְכֵּנוּ תָּמִיד. מִן־הָעוֹלָם וְעַד־הָעוֹלָם אַתָּה אֵל. וּמִבַּלְעָדֶיךָ אֵין לָנוּ מֶלֶךְ גּוֹאֵל וּמוֹשִׁיעַ פּוֹדֶה וּמַצִּיל וּמְפַרְנֵס וּמְרַחֵם בְּכָל־עֵת צָרָה וְצוּקָה אֵידְלָנוּ מֶלֶךְ אֶלָּא אָתָּה: אֱלֹהֵי הָרִאשׁוֹנִים וְהָאַחֲרוֹנִים. אֱלוֹהַּ כָּל־בְּרִיּוֹת אֲדוֹן כָּל־תּוֹלָדוֹת. הַמְהֻלָּל בְּרֹב הַתִּשְׁבָּחוֹת. הַמְנַהֵג עוֹלָמוֹ בְּחֶסֶד וּבְרִיּוֹתָיו בְּרַחֲמִים. וַיְיָ לֹא־יָנוּם וְלֹא־יִישָׁן: הַמְעוֹרֵר יְשֵׁנִים וְהַמֵּקִיץ נִרְדָּמִים וְהַמֵּשִׂיחַ אִלְּמִים וְהַמַּתִּיר אֲסוּרִים וְהַסּוֹמֵךְ נוֹפְלִים וְהַזּוֹקֵף כְּפוּפִים. לְךָ לְבַדְּךָ אֲנַחְנוּ מוֹדִים: אִלּוּ פִינוּ מָלֵא שִׁירָה כַיָּם וּלְשׁוֹנֵנוּ רִנָּה כַּהֲמוֹן גַּלָּיו וְשִׂפְתוֹתֵינוּ שֶׁבַח כְּמֶרְחֲבֵי

THE BREATH OF EVERY LIVING THING

This hymn is the choice of Rabbi Yohanan for the "Benediction of Song" (Pesahim 118a). Its author is unknown. Part of it, however, is already quoted in the Talmud (Berakhot 59b). Much briefer in its original form, later the formula was broadened. A closing blessing after "The Breath of Every Living Thing" concludes the "Benediction of Song."

And slew mighty kings,

               For His mercy endureth for ever:

Sihon king of the Amorites,

               For His mercy endureth for ever;

And Og king of Bashan,

               For His mercy endureth for ever;

And gave their land for a heritage,

               For His mercy endureth for ever;

Even a heritage unto Israel His servant,

               For His mercy endureth for ever.

Who remembered us in our low estate,

               For His mercy endureth for ever;

And hath delivered us from our adversaries,

               For His mercy endureth for ever.

Who giveth food to all flesh,

               For His mercy endureth for ever.

O give thanks unto the God of heaven,

               For His mercy endureth for ever.

THE BREATH OF EVERY LIVING THING

The breath of every living thing shall bless thy name, O Lord our God, and the spirit of all flesh shall glorify and exalt thy memory, our King, for ever. From the eternity of the beginning to the eternity of the end, thou art God, and except for thee we have no redeeming and saving king, liberating and delivering, and provident and compassionate in every time of trouble and distress. We have no king but thee, O God of the first things and the last, God of all creatures, the Lord of all generations, who is lauded with many songs of praise, who conducts his universe with mercy and his creatures with compassion. The Lord slumbers not nor sleeps. It is he who awakens the sleeping, and rouses the slumbering, and makes the dumb converse, and loosens the bound, and steadies the falling, and straightens the bent.

To thee alone do we give thanks. Though our mouth were full of song like the sea, and our tongue of rejoicing like the multitude of its waves, and our lips of praise like the breadth of the horizon, and

רָקִיעַ וְעֵינֵינוּ מְאִירוֹת כַּשֶּׁמֶשׁ וְכַיָּרֵחַ וְיָדֵינוּ פְרוּשׂוֹת כְּנִשְׁרֵי שָׁמַיִם וְרַגְלֵינוּ

קַלּוֹת כָּאַיָּלוֹת. אֵין אֲנַחְנוּ מַסְפִּיקִים לְהוֹדוֹת לְךָ יְיָ אֱלֹהֵינוּ וֵאלֹהֵי

אֲבוֹתֵינוּ וּלְבָרֵךְ אֶת־שְׁמֶךָ עַל־אַחַת מֵאֶלֶף אֶלֶף אַלְפֵי אֲלָפִים וְרִבֵּי

רְבָבוֹת פְּעָמִים הַטּוֹבוֹת שֶׁעָשִׂיתָ עִם־אֲבוֹתֵינוּ וְעִמָּנוּ: מִמִּצְרַיִם גְּאַלְתָּנוּ

יְיָ אֱלֹהֵינוּ וּמִבֵּית עֲבָדִים פְּדִיתָנוּ. בְּרָעָב זַנְתָּנוּ וּבְשָׂבָע כִּלְכַּלְתָּנוּ.

וּמֵחֶרֶב הִצַּלְתָּנוּ וּמִדֶּבֶר מִלַּטְתָּנוּ. וּמֵחֳלָיִם רָעִים וְנֶאֱמָנִים דִּלִּיתָנוּ:

עַד־הֵנָּה עֲזָרוּנוּ רַחֲמֶיךָ. וְלֹא־עֲזָבוּנוּ חֲסָדֶיךָ. וְאַל־תִּטְּשֵׁנוּ יְיָ אֱלֹהֵינוּ

לָנֶצַח: עַל־כֵּן אֵבָרִים שֶׁפִּלַּגְתָּ בָּנוּ וְרוּחַ וּנְשָׁמָה שֶׁנָּפַחְתָּ בְּאַפֵּינוּ וְלָשׁוֹן

אֲשֶׁר שַׂמְתָּ בְּפִינוּ. הֵן הֵם יוֹדוּ וִיבָרְכוּ וִישַׁבְּחוּ וִיפָאֲרוּ וִירוֹמְמוּ וְיַעֲרִיצוּ

וְיַקְדִּישׁוּ וְיַמְלִיכוּ אֶת־שִׁמְךָ מַלְכֵּנוּ: כִּי כָל־פֶּה לְךָ יוֹדֶה. וְכָל־לָשׁוֹן

לְךָ תִשָּׁבַע. וְכָל־בֶּרֶךְ לְךָ תִכְרַע. וְכָל־קוֹמָה לְפָנֶיךָ תִשְׁתַּחֲוֶה. וְכָל־

לְבָבוֹת יִירָאוּךָ. וְכָל־קֶרֶב וּכְלָיוֹת יְזַמְּרוּ לִשְׁמֶךָ. כַּדָּבָר שֶׁכָּתוּב.

כָּל־עַצְמוֹתַי תֹּאמַרְנָה יְיָ מִי כָמוֹךָ. מַצִּיל עָנִי מֵחָזָק מִמֶּנּוּ וְעָנִי וְאֶבְיוֹן

מִגֹּזְלוֹ: מִי יִדְמֶה־לָּךְ וּמִי יִשְׁוֶה־לָּךְ וּמִי יַעֲרָךְ־לָךְ. הָאֵל הַגָּדוֹל הַגִּבּוֹר

וְהַנּוֹרָא אֵל עֶלְיוֹן קֹנֵה שָׁמַיִם וָאָרֶץ: נְהַלֶּלְךָ וּנְשַׁבֵּחֲךָ וּנְפָאֶרְךָ וּנְבָרֵךְ

אֶת־שֵׁם קָדְשֶׁךָ. כָּאָמוּר לְדָוִד בָּרְכִי נַפְשִׁי אֶת־יְיָ וְכָל־קְרָבַי אֶת־שֵׁם

קָדְשׁוֹ:

הָאֵל בְּתַעֲצֻמוֹת עֻזֶּךָ: הַגָּדוֹל בִּכְבוֹד שְׁמֶךָ: הַגִּבּוֹר לָנֶצַח וְהַנּוֹרָא

בְּנוֹרְאוֹתֶיךָ:

הַמֶּלֶךְ הַיּוֹשֵׁב עַל־כִּסֵּא רָם וְנִשָּׂא:

our eyes were shining like the sun and the moon, and our hands were spread like the eagles of the sky, and our feet light as the hinds' — we should never thank thee enough, O Lord our God and God of our fathers, and to bless thy name, for one of the thousands of thousands and myriads of myriads of the good thou hast done with our fathers and us.

From Egypt Thou hast redeemed us, O Lord our God, and from the house of slaves ransomed us, in famine fed us, and in plenty provided us, from the sword saved us, and from the pest delivered us, and from evil and serious illnesses lifted us. Till now thy compassions have helped us, and thy mercies have not deserted us; and may Thou never, O Lord our God, desert us. Therefore, the limbs that thou hast distributed among us, and the spirit and breath that thou hast blown into our nostrils, and the tongue which thou hast placed in our mouths — they shall give thanks, and bless, and extol, and glorify, and exalt, and reverence, and sanctify, and crown thy name, our King.

For every mouth shall give thanks to thee, and every tongue shall swear to thee, and every knee shall kneel to thee, and every stature bow down before thee, and all hearts shall fear thee, the inward parts and reins shall sing to thy name. As it is written: "All my bones shall say: 'Lord, who is like unto Thee, / Who deliverest the poor from him that is too strong for him, / Yea, the poor and the needy from him that spoileth him?' " [Ps. 35:10].

Who is like thee, and who is equal to thee, and who is comparable to thee, the God who is great, mighty, and awesome, God most high, master of heaven and earth? We shall praise thee, and laud thee, and glorify thee, and bless thy holy name. As it is said: "Bless the Lord, O my soul; / And all that is within me, bless His holy name" [Ps. 103:1].

God, in the might of thy power, great in the glory of thy name, mighty forever, and awesome in thy awesome acts.

King, who sits on a high and exalted throne!

שׁוֹכֵן עַד מָרוֹם וְקָדוֹשׁ שְׁמוֹ: וְכָתוּב. רַנְּנוּ צַדִּיקִים בַּיָי לַיְשָׁרִים נָאוָה

תְהִלָּה: בְּפִי יְשָׁרִים תִּתְהַלָּל. וּבְדִבְרֵי צַדִּיקִים תִּתְבָּרַךְ. וּבִלְשׁוֹן חֲסִידִים

תִּתְרוֹמָם. וּבְקֶרֶב קְדוֹשִׁים תִּתְקַדָּשׁ:

וּבְמַקְהֲלוֹת רִבְבוֹת עַמְּךָ בֵּית יִשְׂרָאֵל בְּרִנָּה יִתְפָּאַר שִׁמְךָ מַלְכֵּנוּ

בְּכָל־דּוֹר וָדוֹר: שֶׁכֵּן חוֹבַת כָּל־הַיְצוּרִים לְפָנֶיךָ יְיָ אֱלֹהֵינוּ וֵאלֹהֵי

אֲבוֹתֵינוּ. לְהוֹדוֹת לְהַלֵּל לְשַׁבֵּחַ לְפָאֵר לְרוֹמֵם לְהַדֵּר לְבָרֵךְ לְעַלֵּה

וּלְקַלֵּס עַל־כָּל־דִּבְרֵי שִׁירוֹת וְתִשְׁבְּחוֹת דָּוִד בֶּן־יִשַׁי עַבְדְּךָ מְשִׁיחֶךָ:

יִשְׁתַּבַּח שִׁמְךָ לָעַד מַלְכֵּנוּ הָאֵל הַמֶּלֶךְ הַגָּדוֹל וְהַקָּדוֹשׁ בַּשָּׁמַיִם וּבָאָרֶץ:

כִּי־לְךָ נָאֶה יְיָ אֱלֹהֵינוּ וֵאלֹהֵי אֲבוֹתֵינוּ שִׁיר וּשְׁבָחָה הַלֵּל וְזִמְרָה

עֹז וּמֶמְשָׁלָה נֶצַח גְּדֻלָּה וּגְבוּרָה תְּהִלָּה וְתִפְאֶרֶת קְדֻשָּׁה וּמַלְכוּת

בְּרָכוֹת וְהוֹדָאוֹת מֵעַתָּה וְעַד־עוֹלָם:

בָּרוּךְ אַתָּה יְיָ אֵל מֶלֶךְ גָּדוֹל בַּתִּשְׁבָּחוֹת. אֵל הַהוֹדָאוֹת. אֲדוֹן הַנִּפְלָאוֹת.

הַבּוֹחֵר בְּשִׁירֵי זִמְרָה. מֶלֶךְ אֵל חֵי הָעוֹלָמִים:

The participants lift up their cups of wine and say:

בָּרוּךְ אַתָּה יְיָ אֱלֹהֵינוּ מֶלֶךְ הָעוֹלָם. בּוֹרֵא פְּרִי הַגָּפֶן:

The fourth cup is drunk, while reclining. The following final
blessing is then recited. The words in brackets are added on the
Sabbath.

בָּרוּךְ אַתָּה יְיָ אֱלֹהֵינוּ מֶלֶךְ הָעוֹלָם. עַל־הַגֶּפֶן וְעַל־פְּרִי הַגֶּפֶן. וְעַל

תְּנוּבַת הַשָּׂדֶה וְעַל־אֶרֶץ חֶמְדָּה טוֹבָה וּרְחָבָה שֶׁרָצִיתָ וְהִנְחַלְתָּ לַאֲבוֹתֵינוּ

94

Dweller in eternity — High One and Holy One is his name. And it is written: "Rejoice in the Lord, O ye righteous, / Praise is comely for the upright" [Ps. 33:1]. In the mouth of the upright shalt thou be praised, in the words of the just shalt thou be blessed, in the tongue of the pious shalt thou be exalted, and in the midst of the holy shalt thou be hallowed.

And in the assemblies of the myriads of thy folk, the house of Israel, in joyful song thy name will be glorified, our King, in every generation. For such is the duty of all created things to you, O Lord our God and God of our fathers, to give thanks, to praise, laud, glorify, extol, honor, bless, exalt, and commend more than all the words of the songs and praises of David the son of Jesse, thy servant, thine anointed one.

Praised be thy name for ever our king, God the King, great and holy in heaven and on earth. For unto thee are becoming, O Lord our God and God of our fathers, song and praise, adoration and chant, power and dominion, victory, greatness, and strength, fame and glory, sanctity and sovereignty, blessings and thanksgivings from now until for ever.

Blessed art thou, O Lord, God and King, who art mightily praised, God of thanksgivings, Lord of wonders, who chooses song and psalm, King, God, the life of the world.

The participants lift up their cups of wine and say:

Blessed art thou, O Lord our God, King of the universe, creator of the fruit of the vine.

The fourth cup is drunk, while reclining. The following final blessing is then recited. The words in brackets are added on the Sabbath.

Blessed art thou, O Lord our God, king of the universe, for the vine and for the fruit of the vine, for the yield of the field, and for the land, pleasant, goodly and broad which thou favored and gave as an inheritance to our fathers, to eat of its fruit and to be sated with its goodness.

לֶאֱכוֹל מִפִּרְיָהּ וְלִשְׂבּוֹעַ מִטּוּבָהּ: רַחֵם יְיָ אֱלֹהֵינוּ עַל־יִשְׂרָאֵל עַמֶּךָ וְעַל־יְרוּשָׁלַיִם עִירָךְ. וְעַל־צִיּוֹן מִשְׁכַּן כְּבוֹדֶךָ. וְעַל־מִזְבַּחֲךָ וְעַל־הֵיכָלֶךָ. וּבְנֵה יְרוּשָׁלַיִם עִיר הַקֹּדֶשׁ בִּמְהֵרָה בְיָמֵינוּ. וְהַעֲלֵנוּ לְתוֹכָהּ וְשַׂמְּחֵנוּ בְּבִנְיָנָהּ. וְנֹאכַל מִפִּרְיָהּ וְנִשְׂבַּע מִטּוּבָהּ. וּנְבָרֶכְךָ עָלֶיהָ בִּקְדֻשָׁה וּבְטָהֳרָה: [וּרְצֵה וְהַחֲלִיצֵנוּ בְּיוֹם הַשַּׁבָּת הַזֶּה] וְשַׂמְּחֵנוּ בְּיוֹם חַג הַמַּצּוֹת הַזֶּה. כִּי־אַתָּה יְיָ טוֹב וּמֵטִיב לַכֹּל וְנוֹדֶה לְּךָ עַל הָאָרֶץ וְעַל פְּרִי הַגָּפֶן: בָּרוּךְ אַתָּה יְיָ עַל הָאָרֶץ וְעַל פְּרִי הַגָּפֶן:

נ ר צ ה

חֲסַל סִדּוּר פֶּסַח כְּהִלְכָתוֹ.

כְּכָל־מִשְׁפָּטוֹ וְחֻקָּתוֹ:

כַּאֲשֶׁר זָכִינוּ לְסַדֵּר אוֹתוֹ.

כֵּן נִזְכֶּה לַעֲשׂוֹתוֹ:

זָךְ שׁוֹכֵן מְעוֹנָה.

קוֹמֵם קְהַל מִי מָנָה:

קָרֵב נַהֵל נִטְעֵי כַנָּה.

פְּדוּיִם לְצִיּוֹן בְּרִנָּה:

לְשָׁנָה הַבָּאָה בִּירוּשָׁלָיִם:

Have pity, O Lord our God upon Israel, thy people, upon Jerusalem, thy city, upon Zion, the dwelling of thy glory, upon thine altar and upon thy dwelling place. And build Jerusalem, the city of holiness, speedily and in our days and bring us up into its midst, and cause us to rejoice in its rebuilding; let us eat its fruit and be sated with its goodness and bless thee for it in holiness and purity. [And be it thy will to strengthen us on this Sabbath day.] And make us rejoice upon this Festival of Unleavened Bread. For thou, O Lord art good and do good to all. And we shall thank thee for the land and for the fruit of the vine. Blessed art thou, O Lord, for the land and for the fruit of the vine.

CONCLUDED

Concluded is the Passover Seder,
According to its law and custom.
As we have lived to celebrate it
So may we live to celebrate it again.
Pure One, who dwells in his habitation
Redress the countless congregation.
Speedily lead the offshoots of thy stock
Redeemed, to Zion in joyous song.

NEXT YEAR IN JERUSALEM!

CONCLUDED

An adaptation of a medieval liturgical poem (*kerovah*) intended for recitation on the Sabbath preceding Passover. The author is Rabbi Joseph Tov Elem (11th cent.); in its original form the poem treats the precepts connected with Passover in great detail.

countless congregation: cf. Ps. 76:3 or Deut. 33:27

Redeemed: cf. Ps. 80:16 and Isa. 35:10; 51:11

Next year: Jews in Israel say לְשָׁנָה הַבָּאָה בִּירוּשָׁלַיִם הַבְּנוּיָה (Next year in Jerusalem rebuilt).

At the first Seder service:

וַיְהִי בַּחֲצִי הַלָּיְלָה:

אָז רוֹב נִסִּים הִפְלֵאתָ בַּלָּיְלָה.
בְּרֹאשׁ אַשְׁמוּרוֹת זֶה הַלָּיְלָה.
גֵּר צֶדֶק נִצַּחְתּוֹ כְּנֶחֱלַק לוֹ לָיְלָה.
וַיְהִי בַּחֲצִי הַלָּיְלָה:

דַּנְתָּ מֶלֶךְ גְּרָר בַּחֲלוֹם הַלָּיְלָה.
הִפְחַדְתָּ אֲרַמִּי בְּאֶמֶשׁ לָיְלָה.
וְיִשְׂרָאֵל יָשַׂר לָאֵל וַיּוּכַל לוֹ לָיְלָה.
וַיְהִי בַּחֲצִי הַלָּיְלָה:

זֶרַע בְּכוֹרֵי פַתְרוֹס מָחַצְתָּ בַּחֲצִי הַלָּיְלָה.
חֵילָם לֹא מָצְאוּ בְּקוּמָם בַּלָּיְלָה.
טִיסַת נְגִיד חֲרוֹשֶׁת סִלִּיתָ בְּכוֹכְבֵי לָיְלָה.
וַיְהִי בַּחֲצִי הַלָּיְלָה:

SUPPLEMENTARY HYMNS

It is customary to round out the Seder service by reciting a number of hymns
after the official conclusion. The choice of hymns varies from ritual to ritual;
our Ashkenazic Haggadah ritual has the largest selection of all.

The two following hymns are early medieval liturgical poems which are
recited alternately, one for each of the two Passover Seders. Both poems are
didactic, containing many allusions, which require for their full appreciation a
comprehensive knowledge of biblical and talmudic lore.

The first poem is an excerpt from the liturgy for the Sabbath before Passover
in the Ashkenazic ritual. Composed by the early Palestinian poet Yannai, it
enumerates various significant events which took place, according to the midrashic
interpretation, on Passover night (Numbers Rabbah XX. 12). The poem concludes
with a fervent prayer for the messianic redemption. It is customary to recite the
verse *And so it came to pass in the middle of the night* (cf. Exod. 12:29) as a refrain
after every three strophes. However, the refrain does not belong in the body of
the poem, where it tends to disturb the continuity of the thought. Also, it confuses

At the first Seder service:

And so it came to pass in the middle of the night

It was then You worked many miracles	at night.
At the beginning of the watches	on this night.
You gave victory to the convert when divided was	the night.

And so it came to pass in the middle of the night.

You sentenced the king of Gerar in a dream	of night.
You terrorized the Aramean in the yester	night.
And Israel with an angel fought and he over- came him	at night.

And so it came to pass in the middle of the night.

You crushed the first-born seed of Pathros in the middle	of the night.
They found their strength gone when they rose	at night.
The lord of Harosheth's host were levelled by the stars	of night.

And so it came to pass in the middle of the night.

---

the meaning of the last stanza which is concerned with future rather than past miracles.

it came to pass: cf. Exod. 12:29.

At the beginning: The night is divided into three watches; the first is called *rosh ashmurot* (Lam. 2:19).

convert: Abraham.

divided: during the battle against the four kings (Gen. 14:15).

king of Gerar: Abimelech, who "sent and took" Sarah, after "Abraham said of Sarah, his wife: 'She is my sister' " (Gen. 20:2-3).

the Aramean: Laban, whom God told "yesternight" not to harm Jacob (Gen. 31:29).

Israel: Jacob, whose name was changed to Israel (Gen. 32:25; Hosea 12:5)

Pathros: Egypt (Gen. 10:14; Jer. 44:1).

their strength: their children (Ps. 76:6).

lord of Harosheth: Sisera, the Canaanite general who "dwelt in Harosheth goiim," and was defeated by Deborah and Barak.

the stars: "The stars in their courses fought against Sisera" (Judg. 5:20).

יָעַץ מְחָרֵף לְנוֹפֵף אִוּוּי הוֹבַשְׁתָּ פְגָרָיו בַּלָּיְלָה.

כָּרַע בֵּל וּמַצָּבוֹ בְּאִישׁוֹן לָיְלָה.

לְאִישׁ חֲמוּדוֹת נִגְלָה רָז חֲזוֹת לָיְלָה.

וַיְהִי בַּחֲצִי הַלָּיְלָה:

מִשְׁתַּכֵּר בִּכְלֵי קֹדֶשׁ נֶהֱרַג בּוֹ בַּלָּיְלָה.

נוֹשַׁע מִבּוֹר אֲרָיוֹת פּוֹתֵר בְּעִתּוּתֵי לָיְלָה.

שִׂנְאָה נָטַר אֲגָגִי וְכָתַב סְפָרִים בַּלָּיְלָה.

וַיְהִי בַּחֲצִי הַלָּיְלָה:

עוֹרַרְתָּ נִצְחֲךָ עָלָיו בְּנֶדֶד שְׁנַת-לָיְלָה.

פּוּרָה תִדְרוֹךְ לְשׁוֹמֵר מַה-מִלָּיְלָה.

צָרַח כַּשּׁוֹמֵר וְשָׂח אָתָא בֹקֶר וְגַם-לָיְלָה.

וַיְהִי בַּחֲצִי הַלָּיְלָה:

קָרֵב יוֹם אֲשֶׁר הוּא לֹא יוֹם וְלֹא לָיְלָה.

רָם הוֹדַע כִּי-לְךָ יוֹם אַף-לְךָ הַלָּיְלָה.

שׁוֹמְרִים הַפְקֵד לְעִירְךָ כָּל-הַיּוֹם וְכָל-הַלָּיְלָה.

תָּאִיר כְּאוֹר יוֹם חֶשְׁכַּת לָיְלָה.

וַיְהִי בַּחֲצִי הַלָּיְלָה:

The blasphemer: Sennacherib, King of Assyria who sent a messenger "to taunt the living God" (II Kings 19:4; 22).　　*Chosen*: Zion, the chosen city (Ps. 132:13).

rotted his corpses: "The angel of the Lord went forth and smote in the camp of the Assyrians . . . ." (II Kings 19:35).　　*Bel*: the idol (Dan. 3:1. Cf. Isa. 46:1).

beloved man: Daniel (Dan. 10:11), to whom the interpretation of Nebuchadnezzar's dream was revealed (Dan. 2:19).

grew drunk: Belshazzar, the Babylonian king who "made a great feast for a thousand of his lords" (Dan. 5), at which he drank from the vessels of the Temple in Jerusalem.　　*was slain*: Dan. 5:30.

saved from the lion's den: Daniel (Dan. 6:20).

The blasphemer thought to ravage your Chosen;
    You rotted his corpses   **at night.**
Bel fell and his pedestal in the middle   **of the night.**
To the greatly beloved man was bared the
    secret vision   **of night.**
    And so it came to pass in the middle of the night.

He who grew drunk from the sacred vessels
    was slain   **on that very night.**
He who was saved from the lion's den inter-
    preted dread dreams   **of night.**
The Agagite nurtured hate, and wrote scrolls   **at night.**
    And so it came to pass in the middle of the night.

You began to overpower him when sleep fled   **at night.**
You will trample down the winepress for him
    who asks, "Watchman, what   **of the night?"**
He will sing out like a watchman, saying, "The
    morning cometh and also   **the night."**
    And so it came to pass in the middle of the night.

O, bring near the day that is neither day nor   **night.**
O, Most High, announce, yours the day is, yours **the night.**
Set watchmen to watch your city all the day
    and all   **the night.**
Brighten, like the light of day, the dark   **of night.**
    And so it came to pass in the middle of the night.

The Agagite: Haman who sent letters to the King's provinces to have all the Jews destroyed (Esther 3:13).

when sleep fled: from Ahasuerus (Esther 6:1).

trample down the winepress: i. e., destroy (cf. Isa. 63:3).

for him: For the sake of Israel who asks . . . (Isa. 63:3).

The morning cometh: Isa. 21:12. The question is taken to mean: "When will the deliverance from the oppressor come?" The answer given is "The morning cometh" for you, "and also the night" for your oppressors.

neither day nor night: the day of Messianic deliverance (Zech. 14:7).

yours the day is, yours the night: Ps. 74:16.

Set watchmen: Isa. 62:6.

At the second Seder service:

וַאֲמַרְתֶּם זֶבַח־פֶּסַח:

אֹמֶץ גְּבוּרוֹתֶיךָ הִפְלֵאתָ בַּפֶּסַח.

בְּרֹאשׁ כָּל־מוֹעֲדוֹת נִשֵּׂאתָ פֶּסַח.

גִּלִּיתָ לְאֶזְרָחִי חֲצוֹת לֵיל פֶּסַח.

וַאֲמַרְתֶּם זֶבַח־פֶּסַח:

דְּלָתָיו דָּפַקְתָּ כְּחוֹם הַיּוֹם בַּפֶּסַח.

הִסְעִיד נוֹצְצִים עֻגּוֹת מַצּוֹת בַּפֶּסַח.

וְאֶל־הַבָּקָר רָץ זֵכֶר לְשׁוֹר עֵרֶךְ פֶּסַח.

וַאֲמַרְתֶּם זֶבַח־פֶּסַח:

זוֹעֲמוּ סְדוֹמִים וְלוֹהֲטוּ בָּאֵשׁ בַּפֶּסַח.

חֻלַּץ לוֹט מֵהֶם וּמַצּוֹת אָפָה בְּקֵץ פֶּסַח.

טֵאטֵאתָ אַדְמַת מוֹף וְנוֹף בְּעָבְרְךָ בַּפֶּסַח.

וַאֲמַרְתֶּם זֶבַח־פֶּסַח:

The second hymn was composed by the liturgical poet Eleazar Kalir. There
is a strong similarity between this and the previous poem, and it is probable that
Kalir was influenced by Yannai. The hymn is based on the phrase "Ye shall say:
It is the sacrifice of the Passover," from Exodus (cf. 12:27), which Kalir understood to mean: "Ye shall speak of the Passover festival." Here too the opening
verse from Exod. is customarily repeated as a refrain, although at numerous points
it interrupts the continuity of the poem.

And you shall say: cf. Exod. 12:27.

To the first of all festivals You raised: According to the Mishnah Rosh ha-
Shanah I.1, the first of Nisan is the New Year's Day of the festivals, making
Passover the first in the cycle of holidays.

You revealed Yourself to the Ezrahite: Abraham, so called because of his eastern

At the second Seder service:

And so you shall say: "It is the sacrifice of the Passover."

Your powerful miracles You worked	on Passover.
To the first of all festivals You raised	the Passover.
You revealed Yourself to the Ezrahite on the midnight	of Passover.

And you shall say: "It is the sacrifice of the Passover."

On his door you rapped in the heat of the day	on Passover.
He fed the shining ones unleavened cakes	on Passover.
And to the herd he ran, in memory of the Ox	of Passover.

And you shall say: "It is the sacrifice of the Passover."

The Sodomites felt your ire, and were burned in the
    fire   on Passover.
Lot escaped from them, and baked unleavened bread
    at the end   of Passover.
You swept away the land of Moph and Noph when
    You passed through   on Passover.

And you shall say: "It is the sacrifice of the Passover."

---

origin, to whom God revealed himself on Passover during the Covenant between the Sections, according to one tradition (Pirke de Rabbi Eliezer 28).

the shining ones: the angels, after Ezek. 1:7. The cakes Sarah prepared at Abraham's request (Gen. 18:6) are assumed to have been unleavened.

And to the herd he ran: Gen. 18:7.

in memory of the Ox: the portion from the Torah read on the second day of Passover is designated in the Talmud (Megillah 31a) by its initial word "Ox."

and baked unleavened bread: When he entertained the angels (Gen. 19:3). The poet determines the date (Passover) on the basis of the mention of the unleavened bread — which Lot actually chose because of the short time it required to prepare — or by connecting this event with the visit of the angels to Abraham.

Moph and Noph: Josh. 9:6; Isa. 19:13. These are two names for the same Egyptian city (Memphis). The allusion — as indicated in the phrase *You passed through* — is to the death of the first-born, a subject the poet takes up again in the following line.

יָהּ רֹאשׁ כָּל־אוֹן מָחַצְתָּ בְּלֵיל שָׁמוּר פֶּסַח

כַּבִּיר עַל בֵּן בְּכוֹר פָּסַחְתָּ בְּדַם־פֶּסַח.

לְבִלְתִּי תֵּת מַשְׁחִית לָבֹא בִּפְתָחַי בַּפֶּסַח.

וַאֲמַרְתֶּם זֶבַח־פֶּסַח:

מְסֻגֶּרֶת סֻגְּרָה בְּעִתּוֹתֵי פֶּסַח.

נִשְׁמְדָה מִדְיָן בִּצְלִיל שְׂעוֹרֵי עֹמֶר פֶּסַח.

שֹׂרְפוּ מַשְׁמַנֵּי פוּל וְלוּד בִּיקַד יְקוֹד פֶּסַח.

וַאֲמַרְתֶּם זֶבַח־פֶּסַח:

עוֹד הַיּוֹם בְּנֹב לַעֲמוֹד עַד גָּעָה עוֹנַת פֶּסַח.

פַּס יָד כָּתְבָה לְקַעֲקֵעַ צוּל בַּפֶּסַח.

צָפֹה הַצָּפִית עָרוֹךְ הַשֻּׁלְחָן בַּפֶּסַח.

וַאֲמַרְתֶּם זֶבַח־פֶּסַח:

---

on the watchful night: after Exod. 12:42.

your first-born son: Israel, the first-born son of God, was passed over at the time of the death of "all the first-born in the land of Egypt" (Exod. 12:22).

Not suffering the Destroyer: A literal reminiscence of Exod. 12:23.

The well-barred city: Jericho (Josh. 6:1), which was besieged after the Israelites celebrated the Passover (Josh. 5:10).

Midian destroyed by the barley cake dream: The dream Gideon overheard and interpreted as an indication of the imminent fall of Midian (Judg. 7:13). The cake of barley, although it appeared only in a dream, was identified in the Midrash (Pesikta Rabbati XVIII) as the Omer of the second day of Passover.

God, all the first-born strength You crushed on the
    watchful night   of Passover.

O, Powerful One, your first-born son you passed
    over by the blood   of Passover.

Not suffering the Destroyer to come into our doors   on Passover.

And you shall say: "It is the sacrifice of the Passover."

The well-barred city was unbarred in the season   of Passover.

Midian destroyed by the barley cake dream, the
    Omer offering   of Passover.

The lustiest of Pul and Lud were burned, when the
    fire flamed   on Passover.

And you shall say: "It is the sacrifice of the Passover."

"This very day shall he halt at Nob"; before the
    approach   of Passover.

The palm of the hand wrote on the wall the uprooting
    of Tzul   on Passover.

When the lamps are lit, the table set   on Passover.

And you shall say: "It is the sacrifice of the Passover."

Pul and Lud: Isa. 66:19, here taken to be Assyrian tribes; following the Midrash (Yalkut Shimeoni, Esther 1058), they were destroyed on Passover.

This very day: The reference is to Sennacherib (Isa. 10:32). Nob is in the vicinity of Jerusalem.

The palm of the hand: The hand that wrote the warning: *Mene, mene, tekel upharsin* on the wall at the banquet of Belshazzar (Dan. 5). Babylonia is called Tzulah in the talmudic comment on Isa. 44:27 (Yerushalmi Berakhot 7b).

When the lamps are lit, the table set: The words of the prophet (Isa. 21:5) are understood as an allusion to the revel of Belshazzar.

קָהָל כִּנְּסָה הֲדַסָּה לְשַׁלֵּשׁ צוֹם בַּפֶּסַח.

רֹאשׁ מִבֵּית רָשָׁע מָחַצְתָּ בְּעֵץ חֲמִשִּׁים בַּפֶּסַח.

שְׁתֵּי אֵלֶּה רֶגַע תָּבִיא לְעוּצִית בַּפֶּסַח.

תָּעֹז יָדְךָ תָּרוּם יְמִינְךָ כְּלֵיל הִתְקַדֵּשׁ חַג פֶּסַח.

וַאֲמַרְתֶּם זֶבַח־פֶּסַח:

רָאִיתִי אֶצֶשׂי מַעֲשֵׂה
בְּיִהְגֵי לִטְמֵז הָאֶצְבַּע

Man with a kiddush cup.
Prague, 1526 (JTSAL).

כִּי לוֹ נָאֶה. כִּי לוֹ יָאֶה:

אַדִּיר בִּמְלוּכָה. בָּחוּר כַּהֲלָכָה. גְּדוּדָיו
יֹאמְרוּ לוֹ. לְךָ וּלְךָ. לְךָ כִּי לְךָ. לְךָ
אַף לְךָ. לְךָ יְיָ הַמַּמְלָכָה. כִּי לוֹ נָאֶה. כִּי
לוֹ יָאֶה:

דָּגוּל בִּמְלוּכָה. הָדוּר כַּהֲלָכָה. וָתִיקָיו
יֹאמְרוּ לוֹ. לְךָ וּלְךָ. לְךָ כִּי לְךָ. לְךָ
אַף לְךָ. לְךָ יְיָ הַמַּמְלָכָה. כִּי לוֹ נָאֶה.
כִּי לוֹ יָאֶה:

Hadassah: the Hebrew name for Esther (Esther 2:7). Since the decree of Haman was issued on the thirteenth of Nisan (Esther 3:7), the fast fell on Passover.

You hanged the head: The time is determined on the basis of the tradition that the sleepless night the king spent was the fifteenth of Nisan.

Two things in a moment: The loss of children and widowhood, predicted for Edom (Isa. 47:9). Edom is called Utzit because the Edomites lived in Utz (Lam. 4:21).

Hadassah called an assembly to a three-day fast on Passover.

You hanged the head of the wicked house on a fifty-
cubit tree on Passover.

Two things in a moment you brought upon Utzit on Passover.

Strong be your hand, and your right raised high as
on the night the feast was hallowed on Passover.

And you shall say: "It is the sacrifice of the Passover."

FOR TO HIM PRAISE IS PROPER

For to him praise is proper, for to him praise is due.

Mighty in dominion, select as is right, his troops say to him:
"Yours and yours, yours but yours, yours only yours,
Yours, O Lord, is the kingship."

For to him praise is proper, for to him praise is due.

Dinstinguished in dominion, glorious as is right, his faithful say to
him:
"Yours and yours, yours but yours, yours only yours,
Yours, O Lord, is the kingship."

For to him praise is proper, for to him praise is due.

Strong be your hand: Ps. 89:14.

as on the night the feast was hallowed: when it was originally instituted in
Egypt.

For To Him Praise Is Proper

An ancient popular alphabetical acrostic whose author is unknown. It is
based on Genesis Rabbah VI. 2: " 'Thine is the day, Thine also the night'; to Thee

זַכַּאי בִּמְלוּכָה. חָסִין כַּהֲלָכָה. טַפְסְרָיו יֹאמְרוּ לוֹ. לְךָ וּלְךָ. לְךָ כִּי

לְךָ. לְךָ אַף לְךָ. לְךָ יְיָ הַמַּמְלָכָה. כִּי לוֹ נָאֶה. כִּי לוֹ יָאֶה:

יָחִיד בִּמְלוּכָה. כַּבִּיר כַּהֲלָכָה. לִמּוּדָיו יֹאמְרוּ לוֹ. לְךָ וּלְךָ. לְךָ כִּי

לְךָ. לְךָ אַף לְךָ. לְךָ יְיָ הַמַּמְלָכָה. כִּי לוֹ נָאֶה. כִּי לוֹ יָאֶה:

מָרוֹם בִּמְלוּכָה. נוֹרָא כַּהֲלָכָה. סְבִיבָיו יֹאמְרוּ לוֹ. לְךָ וּלְךָ. לְךָ כִּי

לְךָ. לְךָ אַף לְךָ. לְךָ יְיָ הַמַּמְלָכָה. כִּי לוֹ נָאֶה. כִּי לוֹ יָאֶה:

עָנָיו בִּמְלוּכָה. פּוֹדֶה כַּהֲלָכָה. צַדִּיקָיו יֹאמְרוּ לוֹ. לְךָ וּלְךָ. לְךָ כִּי

לְךָ. לְךָ אַף לְךָ. לְךָ יְיָ הַמַּמְלָכָה. כִּי לוֹ נָאֶה. כִּי לוֹ יָאֶה:

קָדוֹשׁ בִּמְלוּכָה. רַחוּם כַּהֲלָכָה. שִׁנְאַנָּיו יֹאמְרוּ לוֹ. לְךָ וּלְךָ. לְךָ כִּי

לְךָ. לְךָ אַף לְךָ. לְךָ יְיָ הַמַּמְלָכָה. כִּי לוֹ נָאֶה. כִּי לוֹ יָאֶה:

תַּקִּיף בִּמְלוּכָה. תּוֹמֵךְ כַּהֲלָכָה. תְּמִימָיו יֹאמְרוּ לוֹ. לְךָ וּלְךָ. לְךָ כִּי

לְךָ. לְךָ אַף לְךָ. לְךָ יְיָ הַמַּמְלָכָה. כִּי לוֹ נָאֶה. כִּי לוֹ יָאֶה:

---

the day sings praises, to Thee the night sings praises," and makes use of two additional verses (Ps. 65:2; I Chron. 29:11).

Just in dominion, great in substance as is right, his princes say to
 him:
   "Yours and yours, yours but yours, yours only yours,
   Yours, O Lord, is the kingship."
 For to him praise is proper, for to him praise is due.

Sole in dominion, powerful as is right, his disciples say to him:
   "Yours and yours, yours but yours, yours only yours,
   Yours, O Lord, is the kingship."
 For to him praise is proper, for to him praise is due.

High over his dominion, stupendous as is right, those around him
 say to him:
   "Yours and yours, yours but yours, yours only yours,
   Yours, O Lord, is the kingship."
 For to him praise is proper, for to him praise is due.

Modest in dominion, redeemer as is right, his righteous say to him:
   "Yours and yours, yours but yours, yours only yours,
   Yours, O Lord, is the kingship."
 For to him praise is proper, for to him praise is due.

Sacred in dominion, compassionate as is right, his angels say to
 him:
   "Yours and yours, yours but yours, yours only yours,
   Yours, O Lord, is the kingship."
 For to him praise is proper, for to him praise is due.

Strong in dominion, supporter as is right, his pure ones say to
 him:
   "Yours and yours, yours but yours, yours only yours,
   Yours, O Lord, is the kingship."
 For to him praise is proper, for to him praise is due.

אַדִּיר **הוּא**. יִבְנֶה בֵיתוֹ בְּקָרוֹב.

בִּמְהֵרָה. בִּמְהֵרָה. בְּיָמֵינוּ בְּקָרוֹב.

אֵל בְּנֵה. אֵל בְּנֵה. בְּנֵה בֵיתְךָ בְּקָרוֹב:

בָּחוּר **הוּא**. גָּדוֹל **הוּא**. דָּגוּל **הוּא**. יִבְנֶה בֵיתוֹ בְּקָרוֹב.

בִּמְהֵרָה. בִּמְהֵרָה. בְּיָמֵינוּ בְּקָרוֹב.

אֵל בְּנֵה. אֵל בְּנֵה. בְּנֵה בֵיתְךָ בְּקָרוֹב:

הָדוּר **הוּא**. וָתִיק **הוּא**. זַכַּאי **הוּא**. יִבְנֶה בֵיתוֹ בְּקָרוֹב.

בִּמְהֵרָה. בִּמְהֵרָה. בְּיָמֵינוּ בְּקָרוֹב.

אֵל בְּנֵה. אֵל בְּנֵה. בְּנֵה בֵיתְךָ בְּקָרוֹב:

חָסִיד **הוּא**. טָהוֹר **הוּא**. יָחִיד **הוּא**. יִבְנֶה בֵיתוֹ בְּקָרוֹב.

בִּמְהֵרָה. בִּמְהֵרָה. בְּיָמֵינוּ בְּקָרוֹב.

אֵל בְּנֵה. אֵל בְּנֵה. בְּנֵה בֵיתְךָ בְּקָרוֹב:

כַּבִּיר **הוּא**. לָמוּד **הוּא**. מֶלֶךְ **הוּא**. יִבְנֶה בֵיתוֹ בְּקָרוֹב.

בִּמְהֵרָה. בִּמְהֵרָה. בְּיָמֵינוּ בְּקָרוֹב.

אֵל בְּנֵה. אֵל בְּנֵה. בְּנֵה בֵיתְךָ בְּקָרוֹב:

MIGHTY IS HE

This alphabetical acrostic was sung in Germany in the 15th cent., while in Avignon it served as a festival song with no special reference to Passover. This

Mighty is he, he will build his Temple soon.
Speedily, speedily, in our days and soon.
God build, God build, build your Temple soon.

Select is he, great is he, distinguished is he; he will build his Temple
soon.
Speedily, speedily, in our days, and soon.
God build, God build, build your Temple soon.

Glorious is he, ancient is he, just is he; he will build his Temple
soon.
Speedily, speedily, in our days and soon.
God build, God build, build your Temple soon.

Gracious is he, pure is he, sole is he; he will build his Temple
soon.
Speedily, speedily, in our days and soon.
God build, God build, build your Temple soon.

Powerful is he, learned is he, king is he; he will build his Temple
soon.
Speedily, speedily, in our days and soon.
God build, God build, build your Temple soon.

---

hymn was also sung in an old German translation. Both the Hebrew and the
German versions are found in the Haggadah of Gershon Kohen, 1526. Many of
the divine attributes cited correspond to those in the preceding hymn, *ki lo naeh*.
We find similar poems elsewhere (e. g., *yavo addir* in Mahzor Romania; and a
Hebrew-Yiddish version among the songs for the Torah procession on Simhat
Torah, in the Polish editions of the Mahzor).

נָאוֹר הוּא. סַגִּיב הוּא. עִוּוּז הוּא. יִבְנֶה בֵּיתוֹ בְּקָרוֹב.

בִּמְהֵרָה. בִּמְהֵרָה. בְּיָמֵינוּ בְּקָרוֹב.

אֵל בְּנֵה. אֵל בְּנֵה. בְּנֵה בֵיתְךָ בְּקָרוֹב:

פּוֹדֶה הוּא. צַדִּיק הוּא. קָדוֹשׁ הוּא. יִבְנֶה בֵּיתוֹ בְּקָרוֹב.

בִּמְהֵרָה. בִּמְהֵרָה. בְּיָמֵינוּ בְּקָרוֹב.

אֵל בְּנֵה. אֵל בְּנֵה. בְּנֵה בֵיתְךָ בְּקָרוֹב:

רַחוּם הוּא. שַׁדַּי הוּא. תַּקִּיף הוּא. יִבְנֶה בֵּיתוֹ בְּקָרוֹב.

בִּמְהֵרָה. בִּמְהֵרָה. בְּיָמֵינוּ בְּקָרוֹב.

אֵל בְּנֵה. אֵל בְּנֵה. בְּנֵה בֵיתְךָ בְּקָרוֹב:

At the second Seder service:

בָּרוּךְ אַתָּה יְיָ אֱלֹהֵינוּ מֶלֶךְ הָעוֹלָם אֲשֶׁר קִדְּשָׁנוּ בְּמִצְוֹתָיו וְצִוָּנוּ עַל סְפִירַת הָעֹמֶר:

הַיּוֹם יוֹם אֶחָד לָעֹמֶר:

יְהִי רָצוֹן מִלְּפָנֶיךָ יְיָ אֱלֹהֵינוּ וֵאלֹהֵי אֲבוֹתֵינוּ שֶׁיִּבָּנֶה בֵּית הַמִּקְדָּשׁ בִּמְהֵרָה בְיָמֵינוּ וְתֵן חֶלְקֵנוּ בְּתוֹרָתֶךָ:

COUNTING OF THE OMER

On the second evening of Passover there begins the counting of the Omer, that is, the counting of the 49 days after the sheaf (Hebrew, *omer*) of barley has

Stupendous is he, overpowering is he, heroic is he; he will build his
 Temple soon.
Speedily, speedily, in our days and soon.
God build, God build, build your Temple soon.

Redeemer is he, righteous is he, sacred is he; he will build his Temple
 soon.
Speedily, speedily, in our days and soon.
God build, God build, build your Temple soon.

Compassionate is he, forceful is he, strong is he; he will build his
 Temple soon.
Speedily, speedily, in our days and soon.
God build, God build, build your Temple soon.

At the second Seder service:

COUNTING OF THE OMER

Blessed art thou, O Lord our God, king of the universe, who sanctified us with his commandments and commanded us concerning the counting of the Omer.

TODAY IS THE FIRST DAY OF THE OMER.

May it be thy will, O Lord our God and God of our fathers, that thy holy Temple shall be rebuilt speedily in our days, and grant us a share in thy Torah.

---

been offered (Lev. 23:10–14). The 49 days extend between Passover and Shavuot, the Feast of Weeks. According to custom, the first counting is recited at a late hour, since the Omer was reaped and prepared only at night.

אֶחָד מִי יוֹדֵעַ. אֶחָד אֲנִי יוֹדֵעַ. אֶחָד אֱלֹהֵינוּ שֶׁבַּשָּׁמַיִם וּבָאָרֶץ:

שְׁנַיִם מִי יוֹדֵעַ. שְׁנַיִם אֲנִי יוֹדֵעַ. שְׁנֵי לֻחוֹת הַבְּרִית. אֶחָד אֱלֹהֵינוּ שֶׁבַּשָּׁמַיִם וּבָאָרֶץ:

שְׁלֹשָׁה מִי יוֹדֵעַ. שְׁלֹשָׁה אֲנִי יוֹדֵעַ. שְׁלֹשָׁה אָבוֹת. שְׁנֵי לֻחוֹת הַבְּרִית. אֶחָד אֱלֹהֵינוּ שֶׁבַּשָּׁמַיִם וּבָאָרֶץ:

אַרְבַּע מִי יוֹדֵעַ. אַרְבַּע אֲנִי יוֹדֵעַ. אַרְבַּע אִמָּהוֹת. שְׁלֹשָׁה אָבוֹת. שְׁנֵי לֻחוֹת הַבְּרִית. אֶחָד אֱלֹהֵינוּ שֶׁבַּשָּׁמַיִם וּבָאָרֶץ:

חֲמִשָּׁה מִי יוֹדֵעַ. חֲמִשָּׁה אֲנִי יוֹדֵעַ. חֲמִשָּׁה חֻמְשֵׁי תוֹרָה. אַרְבַּע אִמָּהוֹת. שְׁלֹשָׁה אָבוֹת. שְׁנֵי לֻחוֹת הַבְּרִית. אֶחָד אֱלֹהֵינוּ שֶׁבַּשָּׁמַיִם וּבָאָרֶץ:

שִׁשָּׁה מִי יוֹדֵעַ. שִׁשָּׁה אֲנִי יוֹדֵעַ. שִׁשָּׁה סִדְרֵי מִשְׁנָה. חֲמִשָּׁה חֻמְשֵׁי תוֹרָה. אַרְבַּע אִמָּהוֹת. שְׁלֹשָׁה אָבוֹת. שְׁנֵי לֻחוֹת הַבְּרִית. אֶחָד אֱלֹהֵינוּ שֶׁבַּשָּׁמַיִם וּבָאָרֶץ:

שִׁבְעָה מִי יוֹדֵעַ. שִׁבְעָה אֲנִי יוֹדֵעַ. שִׁבְעָה יְמֵי שַׁבַּתָּא. שִׁשָּׁה סִדְרֵי מִשְׁנָה. חֲמִשָּׁה חֻמְשֵׁי תוֹרָה. אַרְבַּע אִמָּהוֹת. שְׁלֹשָׁה אָבוֹת. שְׁנֵי לֻחוֹת הַבְּרִית. אֶחָד אֱלֹהֵינוּ שֶׁבַּשָּׁמַיִם וּבָאָרֶץ:

שְׁמוֹנָה מִי יוֹדֵעַ. שְׁמוֹנָה אֲנִי יוֹדֵעַ. שְׁמוֹנָה יְמֵי מִילָה. שִׁבְעָה יְמֵי שַׁבַּתָּא. שִׁשָּׁה סִדְרֵי מִשְׁנָה. חֲמִשָּׁה חֻמְשֵׁי תוֹרָה. אַרְבַּע אִמָּהוֹת. שְׁלֹשָׁה אָבוֹת. שְׁנֵי לֻחוֹת הַבְּרִית. אֶחָד אֱלֹהֵינוּ שֶׁבַּשָּׁמַיִם וּבָאָרֶץ:

WHO KNOWS ONE

Probably composed in the 15th or 16th cent., on a German model, this poem is in the form of questions and answers on the numbers one to thirteen, for which

On both Seder services:

WHO KNOWS ONE

One — who knows one?
> One — I know one.
>> One is our God, who is in heaven and on earth.

Two — who knows two?
> Two — I know two.
>> Two are the tablets of the Covenant,
>> One is our God, who is in heaven and on earth.

Three — who knows three?
> Three — I know three.
>> Three are the Fathers,
>> Two are the tablets of the Covenant, etc.

Four — who knows four?
> Four — I know four.
>> Four are the Mothers,
>> Three are the Fathers, etc.

Five — who knows five?
> Five — I know five.
>> Five are the books of Moses,
>> Four are the Mothers, etc.

Six — who knows six?
> Six — I know six.
>> Six are the Mishnah sections,
>> Five are the books of Moses, etc.

Seven — who knows seven?
> Seven — I know seven.
>> Seven are the days in the week,
>> Six are the Mishnah sections, etc.

---

objects significant in Jewish life had to be found. It was intended to divert the children and keep them from falling asleep during the Seder. In Ceylon and Cochin

תִּשְׁעָה מִי יוֹדֵעַ. תִּשְׁעָה אֲנִי יוֹדֵעַ. תִּשְׁעָה יַרְחֵי לֵדָה. שְׁמוֹנָה יְמֵי מִילָה. שִׁבְעָה יְמֵי שַׁבַּתָּא. שִׁשָּׁה סִדְרֵי מִשְׁנָה. חֲמִשָּׁה חֻמְשֵׁי תוֹרָה. אַרְבַּע אִמָּהוֹת. שְׁלֹשָׁה אָבוֹת. שְׁנֵי לֻחוֹת הַבְּרִית. אֶחָד אֱלֹהֵינוּ שֶׁבַּשָּׁמַיִם וּבָאָרֶץ:

עֲשָׂרָה מִי יוֹדֵעַ. עֲשָׂרָה אֲנִי יוֹדֵעַ. עֲשָׂרָה דִבְּרַיָּא. תִּשְׁעָה יַרְחֵי לֵדָה. שְׁמוֹנָה יְמֵי מִילָה. שִׁבְעָה יְמֵי שַׁבַּתָּא. שִׁשָּׁה סִדְרֵי מִשְׁנָה. חֲמִשָּׁה חֻמְשֵׁי תוֹרָה. אַרְבַּע אִמָּהוֹת. שְׁלֹשָׁה אָבוֹת. שְׁנֵי לֻחוֹת הַבְּרִית. אֶחָד אֱלֹהֵינוּ שֶׁבַּשָּׁמַיִם וּבָאָרֶץ:

אַחַד עָשָׂר מִי יוֹדֵעַ. אַחַד עָשָׂר אֲנִי יוֹדֵעַ. אַחַד עָשָׂר כּוֹכְבַיָּא. עֲשָׂרָה דִבְּרַיָּא. תִּשְׁעָה יַרְחֵי לֵדָה. שְׁמוֹנָה יְמֵי מִילָה. שִׁבְעָה יְמֵי שַׁבַּתָּא. שִׁשָּׁה סִדְרֵי מִשְׁנָה. חֲמִשָּׁה חֻמְשֵׁי תוֹרָה. אַרְבַּע אִמָּהוֹת. שְׁלֹשָׁה אָבוֹת. שְׁנֵי לֻחוֹת הַבְּרִית. אֶחָד אֱלֹהֵינוּ שֶׁבַּשָּׁמַיִם וּבָאָרֶץ:

שְׁנֵים עָשָׂר מִי יוֹדֵעַ. שְׁנֵים עָשָׂר אֲנִי יוֹדֵעַ. שְׁנֵים עָשָׂר שִׁבְטַיָּא. אַחַד עָשָׂר כּוֹכְבַיָּא. עֲשָׂרָה דִבְּרַיָּא. תִּשְׁעָה יַרְחֵי לֵדָה. שְׁמוֹנָה יְמֵי מִילָה. שִׁבְעָה יְמֵי שַׁבַּתָּא. שִׁשָּׁה סִדְרֵי מִשְׁנָה. חֲמִשָּׁה חֻמְשֵׁי תוֹרָה. אַרְבַּע אִמָּהוֹת. שְׁלֹשָׁה אָבוֹת. שְׁנֵי לֻחוֹת הַבְּרִית. אֶחָד אֱלֹהֵינוּ שֶׁבַּשָּׁמַיִם וּבָאָרֶץ:

שְׁלֹשָׁה עָשָׂר מִי יוֹדֵעַ. שְׁלֹשָׁה עָשָׂר אֲנִי יוֹדֵעַ. שְׁלֹשָׁה עָשָׂר מִדַּיָּא. שְׁנֵים עָשָׂר שִׁבְטַיָּא. אַחַד עָשָׂר כּוֹכְבַיָּא. עֲשָׂרָה דִבְּרַיָּא. תִּשְׁעָה יַרְחֵי לֵדָה. שְׁמוֹנָה יְמֵי מִילָה. שִׁבְעָה יְמֵי שַׁבַּתָּא. שִׁשָּׁה סִדְרֵי מִשְׁנָה. חֲמִשָּׁה חֻמְשֵׁי תוֹרָה. אַרְבַּע אִמָּהוֹת. שְׁלֹשָׁה אָבוֹת. שְׁנֵי לֻחוֹת הַבְּרִית. אֶחָד אֱלֹהֵינוּ שֶׁבַּשָּׁמַיִם וּבָאָרֶץ:

---

it is generally sung — in varying and partially corrupt forms — at the table on the Sabbath of the wedding week. The Aramaic forms are employed simply for the sake of the rhyme.

Eight — who knows eight?
>Eight — I know eight.
>>Eight days till circumcision,
>>Seven are the days in the week, etc.

Nine — who knows nine?
>Nine — I know nine.
>>Nine are the months of pregnancy,
>>Eight days till circumcision, etc.

Ten — who knows ten?
>Ten — I know ten.
>>Ten are the Ten Commandments,
>>Nine are the months of pregnancy, etc.

Eleven — who knows eleven?
>Eleven — I know eleven.
>>Eleven are the stars in Joseph's dream,
>>Ten are the Ten Commandments, etc.

Twelve — who knows twelve?
>Twelve — I know twelve.
>>Twelve are the tribes of Israel,
>>Eleven are the stars in Joseph's dream, etc.

Thirteen — who knows thirteen?
>Thirteen — I know thirteen.
>>Thirteen are God's attributes,
>>Twelve are the tribes of Israel, eleven are the stars in Joseph's dream, ten are the Ten Commandments, nine are the months of pregnancy, eight days till circumcision, seven are the days in the week, six are the Mishnah sections, five are the books of Moses, four are the Mothers, three are the Fathers, two are the tablets of the Covenant, one is our God, who is in heaven and on earth.

חַד גַּדְיָא חַד גַּדְיָא. דְּזַבֵּן אַבָּא בִּתְרֵי זוּזֵי.

חַד גַּדְיָא חַד גַּדְיָא:

וְאָתָא שׁוּנְרָא. וְאָכְלָה לְגַדְיָא. דְּזַבֵּן אַבָּא בִּתְרֵי זוּזֵי.

חַד גַּדְיָא חַד גַּדְיָא:

וְאָתָא כַלְבָּא. וְנָשַׁךְ לְשׁוּנְרָא. דְּאָכְלָה לְגַדְיָא. דְּזַבֵּן אַבָּא בִּתְרֵי זוּזֵי.

חַד גַּדְיָא חַד גַּדְיָא:

וְאָתָא חוּטְרָא. וְהִכָּה לְכַלְבָּא. דְּנָשַׁךְ לְשׁוּנְרָא. דְּאָכְלָה לְגַדְיָא. דְּזַבֵּן
אַבָּא בִּתְרֵי זוּזֵי.

חַד גַּדְיָא חַד גַּדְיָא:

וְאָתָא נוּרָא. וְשָׂרַף לְחוּטְרָא. דְּהִכָּה לְכַלְבָּא. דְּנָשַׁךְ לְשׁוּנְרָא. דְּאָכְלָה
לְגַדְיָא. דְּזַבֵּן אַבָּא בִּתְרֵי זוּזֵי.

חַד גַּדְיָא חַד גַּדְיָא:

וְאָתָא מַיָּא. וְכָבָה לְנוּרָא. דְּשָׂרַף לְחוּטְרָא. דְּהִכָּה לְכַלְבָּא. דְּנָשַׁךְ
לְשׁוּנְרָא. דְּאָכְלָה לְגַדְיָא. דְּזַבֵּן אַבָּא בִּתְרֵי זוּזֵי.

חַד גַּדְיָא חַד גַּדְיָא:

וְאָתָא תוֹרָא. וְשָׁתָא לְמַיָּא. דְּכָבָה לְנוּרָא. דְּשָׂרַף לְחוּטְרָא. דְּהִכָּה
לְכַלְבָּא. דְּנָשַׁךְ לְשׁוּנְרָא. דְּאָכְלָה לְגַדְיָא. דְּזַבֵּן אַבָּא בִּתְרֵי זוּזֵי.

חַד גַּדְיָא חַד גַּדְיָא:

The one kid, the one kid, that daddy bought for two zuzim, the one kid.

And the cat came and ate the kid, that daddy bought for two zuzim, the one kid, the one kid.

And the dog came and bit the cat, that ate the kid, etc.

And the stick came and beat the dog, that bit the cat, etc.

And the fire came and burned the stick, that beat the dog, etc.

And the water came and put out the fire, that burned the stick, etc.

And the ox came and drank up the water that put out the fire, etc.

THE ONE KID

This poem written in poor Aramaic with a scattering of Hebrew words, was composed no earlier than the 15th cent. It is reminiscent of certain types of medieval German folk songs. Its theme is already expressed in Eccles. 5:7: "If thou seest the oppression of the poor, and the violent perverting of justice and righteousness in the state, marvel not at the matter; for one higher than the high watcheth, and there are higher than they." It is also contained in the saying of Hillel (Avot II.7): "Because you drowned others, you have been drowned, and in the end they that drowned you shall be drowned." The relation of the poem to the Seder is not clear; it was probably inserted to maintain the interest of the children. It has been the subject of many interpretations, one of the better known allegorical explanations being as follows: Israel is the kid which God bought for two zuzim, which are the two tablets of the Covenant. Subsequently, Israel fell prey to the first of a series of empires, each of which destroyed its predecessor in turn. The cat is Assyria, the dog Babylonia, the stick Persia, the fire Macedonia, the water Rome, the ox the Saracens, the slaughterer the crusaders, and the Angel of Death the Turks.

וְאָתָא הַשּׁוֹחֵט. וְשָׁחַט לְתוֹרָא. דְּשָׁתָא לְמַיָא. דְּכָבָה לְנוּרָא. דְּשָׂרַף לְחוּטְרָא. דְּהִכָּה לְכַלְבָּא. דְּנָשַׁךְ לְשׁוּנְרָא. דְּאָכְלָה לְגַדְיָא. דְּזַבֵּן אַבָּא בִּתְרֵי זוּזֵי.

חַד גַּדְיָא חַד גַּדְיָא:

וְאָתָא מַלְאַךְ הַמָּוֶת. וְשָׁחַט לְשׁוֹחֵט. דְּשָׁחַט לְתוֹרָא. דְּשָׁתָא לְמַיָא. דְּכָבָה לְנוּרָא. דְּשָׂרַף לְחוּטְרָא. דְּהִכָּה לְכַלְבָּא. דְּנָשַׁךְ לְשׁוּנְרָא. דְּאָכְלָה לְגַדְיָא. דְּזַבֵּן אַבָּא בִּתְרֵי זוּזֵי.

חַד גַּדְיָא חַד גַּדְיָא:

וְאָתָא הַקָּדוֹשׁ בָּרוּךְ הוּא. וְשָׁחַט לְמַלְאַךְ הַמָּוֶת. דְּשָׁחַט לְשׁוֹחֵט. דְּשָׁחַט לְתוֹרָא. דְּשָׁתָא לְמַיָא. דְּכָבָה לְנוּרָא. דְּשָׂרַף לְחוּטְרָא. דְּהִכָּה לְכַלְבָּא. דְּנָשַׁךְ לְשׁוּנְרָא. דְּאָכְלָה לְגַדְיָא. דְּזַבֵּן אַבָּא בִּתְרֵי זוּזֵי.

חַד גַּדְיָא חַד גַּדְיָא:

And the butcher came, and butchered the ox, that drank up the water, etc.

And the Angel of Death came and slaughtered the butcher, who butchered the ox, etc.

And the Holy One, blessed be he, came and slaughtered the Angel of Death, who slaughtered the butcher, who butchered the ox, who drank up the water, that put out the fire, that burned the stick, that beat the dog, that bit the cat, that ate the kid, that daddy bought for two zuzim, the one kid, the one kid.

The End

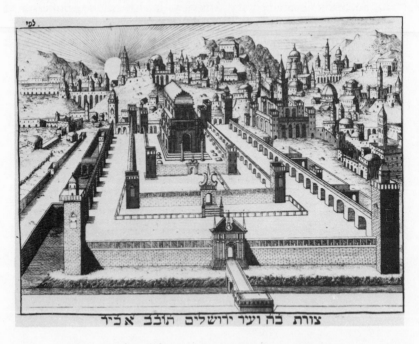

The Holy Temple and the city of Jerusalem in the Messianic age.
Amsterdam, Netherlands, 1712 (JTSAL).